MW00851747

Revised & Expanded 2nd Edition

# BLENKO

## cool
## 50s & 60s glass

Leslie Piña
Photography by Leslie & Ramón Piña

Timberland Regional Library
Service Center
415 Tumwater Blvd. SW
Tumwater, WA 98501

FEB 27 '06

Schiffer Publishing Ltd

4880 Lower Valley Road, Atglen, PA 19310 USA

*dedicated to the designers and*
*makers of cool '50s & '60s glass*

Published by Schiffer Publishing Ltd.
4880 Lower Valley Road
Atglen, PA 19310
Phone: (610) 593-1777; Fax: (610) 593-2002
E-mail: Info@schifferbooks.com

For the largest selection of fine reference books on this and related subjects,
please visit our web site at **www.schifferbooks.com**
We are always looking for people to write books on new and related subjects.
If you have an idea for a book please contact us at the above address.

This book may be purchased from the publisher.
Include $3.95 for shipping.
Please try your bookstore first.
You may write for a free catalog.

In Europe, Schiffer books are distributed by
Bushwood Books
6 Marksbury Ave.
Kew Gardens
Surrey TW9 4JF England
Phone: 44 (0) 20 8392-8585; Fax: 44 (0) 20 8392-9876
E-mail: info@bushwoodbooks.co.uk
Free postage in the U.K., Europe; air mail at cost.

Copyright © 2005 by Leslie Piña
Library of Congress Control Number: 2005931224

All rights reserved. No part of this work may be reproduced or used in
any form or by any means—graphic, electronic, or mechanical, including
photocopying or information storage and retrieval systems—without written
permission from the publisher.
The scanning, uploading and distribution of this book or any part thereof
via the Internet or via any other means without the permission of the publisher is illegal and punishable by law. Please purchase only authorized
editions and do not participate in or encourage the electronic piracy of
copyrighted materials.
"Schiffer," "Schiffer Publishing Ltd. & Design," and the "Design of pen
and ink well" are registered trademarks of Schiffer Publishing Ltd.

Designed by Leslie Piña
Type set in ZapfHumnst Dm BT/Korinna BT

ISBN: 0-7643-2250-8
Printed in China

# Contents

Foreword                                4
Acknowledgments                         5
Introduction                            6
Chronology                              8

## Part One—The Designers
Chapter 1. Winslow Anderson            26
Chapter 2. Wayne Husted                33
Chapter 3. Joel Myers                  41

## Part Two—The Glass
Chapter 4. Stoppers                    48
Chapter 5. Vases                       79
Chapter 6. Handles                    122
Chapter 7. Drinkware                  140
Chapter 8. Tableware                  159
Chapter 9. Lighting                   170
Chapter 10. Figural & Others          180

## Part Three—Past, Present, & Future
Chapter 11. Past: 1960 Catalog        195
Chapter 12. Present: Matt Carter       199
Chapter 13. Future                    206

Bibliography                          207
Designer Index                        208

# Foreword

*by Richard Blenko, Winslow Anderson, Wayne Husted, and Joel Myers*

The history of Blenko Glass Company is that of the "American dream." An Englishman, at the age of sixty-seven fails three times and tries a fourth time. At age sixty-nine, William John Blenko convinces his son to join him in the company not long out of World War I. Four generations later, Blenko is still surviving and influencing American and European design. The vision of son and second generation William H. Blenko Sr. provided a fertile ground for American Studio Glass and provided art glass for America in a production setting. This is the legacy of the Blenko family. The future is unknown for this dinosaur-like operation, but art never dies and good design lives forever. I hope our place in history is assured and a tribute to the many hundreds of people who worked at Blenko these past one hundred years.

*—Richard Deakin Blenko, fourth generation president, July 15, 1999*

During my job interview with Mr. Blenko Sr. in the fall of 1946, I told him that I was curious as to why he needed a designer at all—that I thought the product was very handsome as it was. He was pleased, of course, and explained to me that he and one of his sales representatives met once a year to put the new year's line together. They often had samples of glassware from other companies, many of which were of European manufacture. They did not literally copy their items, but altered them just enough to avoid being accused of copying. Mr. Blenko said that he was only considering a designer to relieve himself of that burdensome task.

I arrived for work in July of 1947, was given a complete tour of the factory, and was introduced to all the employees. After a week of this, Mr. Blenko left suddenly for a few months visit to Europe. Before leaving he said to me, in a most jovial manner, "Well, you're on your own—the place is yours. Do what you want. All I want is a new line of items. Good luck, I'll see you in the fall."

*—Winslow Anderson, June 30, 1999*

The years I spent at Blenko seem like they were in another lifetime. Each year for ten years, I created fifty to sixty designs in time for an annual sales meeting in November. All of the Blenko sales agents would assemble to accept or reject the designs that were submitted—a ritual established before my arrival at Blenko, and I believe, one still followed today. It was somewhat ironic that Bill Blenko Sr. did not claim or appear to have strong opinions about specific designs. To my memory, he never even suggested that a design was too bad, or extreme, or unfinished, or whatever, to show to his salesmen. In fact, it was not uncommon for him to point to a batch of glassware that had been set aside because it was not quite right in shape and say abruptly, "Ship those!" Looking back, I think he knew more than I did that variations were not only endemic to handmade glass, but often enhanced its value. This kind of wisdom combined with a non-judgmental attitude about design made it work.

*—Wayne Husted, July 26, 1999*

From the first moment I walked into the "hot shop" of Blenko Glass Company I knew that I was being given a unique life's opportunity to discover, at nose length, the secrets of hand-made glass. So, in June 1963, I accepted the position as Director of Design. My object in accepting this position was different than my two predecessors in one regard: I was not following, solely, a professional career as an industrial designer. I was, in fact, more interested in learning about all aspects of glass making so that I could train myself to become a skillful, professional glass craftsman-artist. Happily, I was able to achieve my goal during my seven-year tenure at Blenko and have continued a career as an artist and educator in the field of creative glass for the past twenty-nine years. I owe a debt of gratitude to Mr. Blenko Sr. and Mr. Blenko Jr. for allowing me to pursue my goals in the seven years I worked for them. They allowed me a breath of freedom seldom seen in the context of industrial production.

*—Joel Myers, December 15, 1999*

# Acknowledgments to the Second Edition

My thanks to collector and dear friend Gordon Harrell for providing corrections to the first edition, for compiling a list of Blenko colors, and for waiting patiently for the sun to shine over Manhattan so he could shoot beautiful photos just for this book. Thanks also to Carol Seman for letting me photograph the three-lobed bowl before she sold it on Ebay.

# Acknowledgments

Personally meeting the contributors is part of the reward in undertaking a project such as this. During my visits to Milton and to Huntington, West Virginia, while working on *Color Along the River*, I became acquainted with many of the wonderful people who so generously assisted me with this book. Among them are Richard Blenko, Winslow Anderson, and Chris Hatten. Richard is responsible for protecting and sharing the fragile documents and for the displays of Blenko history; Chris does a similar service in his position as librarian at the Huntington Museum; of course, Winslow Anderson is as colorful as ever, and his stories are as fresh and delightful as before. Eason Eige, though no longer curator at the Huntington Museum of Art, still has a presence, and I am grateful for his earlier insights and inspiration.

I would like to thank two new friends for their participation—Wayne Husted, the cool fifties designer, and Matthew Carter, a new talent for a different era. Our visit to Milton would not have been the same if Wayne hadn't flown in from San Francisco or if Matt hadn't hung out with us and made us feel at home at Blenko. They both provided material, insights, and plenty of laughs.

Though I regret not having the pleasure of meeting him personally, thanks to Joel Myers (as well as to Richard, Wayne, and Winslow) for the introductory remarks in the Foreword, and for lending photos of his work.

Thanks to the West Virginia Highway Department for great roads through scenic vistas and 70 mph speed limits. Once again, thanks to the libraries at the Huntington Museum of Art, the Corning Museum of Glass, and Ursuline College; to the Attenson family of antique dealers in Cleveland Heights—Mitchell, Christina, Patricia, and Stuart—for having the foresight to collect some great Blenko pieces and for allowing us to photograph them, as well as to Shannon Demint, Michael Ellison, William Emmerson of Emmerson Troop in Los Angeles, Myra Fortlage, Shirley Friedland, Darlene Jupp, Ken Jupp, and Ara Tavitian of Retro Gallery in Los Angeles. Thanks to all the nice people on Ebay who sold us many of the cool pieces needed to round out the West Virginia collections. And again, thanks to Peter and Nancy Schiffer, Jennifer Lindbeck, and the gang at Schiffer Publishing.

# Introduction

Fifties and sixties glass means more than the two decades for which it is named; the words have also come to represent a *style*. European glass, especially from Italy and Scandinavia, has defined this style by a number of distinctive features—designer-driven; hand-blown; innovative, often sculptural form, such as typically mid-century biomorphic and other freeform shapes; clear vibrant spectrum colors; minimal or no surface embellishment, but often internal hot decoration; emphasis on both design and technical virtuosity; diminished regard for function; little or no regard for historicism; visual representation of adventuresome spirit, even a conscious lack of restraint. The list can go on, but the point is that this mid-century phenomenon, in all its wild variety, is recognizable and even definable.

American glass has not been prominent or even included in either this definition or elite club of European designers and companies. Before the studio movement of the 1960s, American glass had not entered the international modern arena—unless Tiffany's Art Nouveau *favrile* glass and Carder's work at Steuben around the turn of the twentieth century are considered modern. Tiffany and Carder, exceptional, yet almost isolated, examples of artistic excellence were followed in the 1920s and 1930s by a limited number of Art Deco designs by various manufacturers of "Depression Era" production glass. Though modern, and often quite striking, they were molded, mass-produced, and relatively colorless. They were also the exception rather than the rule. Even as late as mid-century, most of the American decorative glass industry remained focused on historic reproductions and interpretations or unremarkable and bland "modern" style. The rest of the industry was primarily in the business of making styleless utilitarian glass.

*Enter Blenko.* From a tradition of brilliantly-colored handmade sheet glass for architectural installations, Blenko had already made a decision to branch out into equally colorful hand-blown decorative tableware. Soon after their initial success, and like their European contemporaries, they hired a professional designer. Blenko's pioneering spirit, plus the traditional skills and color chemistry that were already in place, resulted in a slightly different approach to fifties and sixties glass. Neither made in limited editions nor signed by the designer, lacking internal decoration, and rarely using more than a single color, this glass still had the same flavor—the same spirit—as its more expensive (and perhaps more serious) Italian and Scandinavian counterparts. When Blenko hired Wayne Husted and immediately shifted its focus away from functional tableware, they also invented "cool" American fifties and sixties glass. And most of the other West Virginia companies began to follow their lead, though more often by imitation than by innovation.

William H. Blenko Sr. in his office.

The story of Blenko's early history has already been told in a delightful book by Eason Eige and Rick Wilson in 1987 and later in a fascinating documentary video by Witek & Novak in 1998. In both sources the early years of problems and solutions, failures and successes, of making stained glass, Colonial Williamsburg reproductions, and colorful tableware have been carefully recorded and well-illustrated. A brief chronology following this introduction summarizes some of the highlights of this history. And a catalog reprint for the years 1962-1971 is available as a companion volume to this book.

A word about values might be warranted here, because in the time between the printing of the catalogs and this book, many prices have already changed. Not surprisingly, they have risen, and some of the most desirable designs have risen dramatically in a short span of time. With the added emotional element of competitive bidding, on-line auctions have realized some of the higher prices for Blenko. Whether these represent unique occurrences or a trend has yet to be seen, I have chosen to disregard some of the extreme examples. Like judges of sports competitions who throw out the highest and lowest scores, I have thrown out both the highest and lowest prices in order to present a more typical and realistic range.

In addition to market trends, prices are influenced by things like rarity, design, quality, size, color, finish, and signature. Rarity can be due to short production run or low survival rate—some extreme designs may be more subject to damage or even disposal. Limited production is a more controlled cause of scarcity, especially since it was not unusual to discontinue a design after only one or two years. Either it didn't sell well, or it was too costly to produce. Some designs, even if they stayed in the line for years, command high prices, such as early items with applied leaves, rings, and spirals. Even though the first two digits in the item number indicate the year of introduction (usually the year after it was designed), it is difficult or impossible to identify the actual year of production for enduring designs. If a piece has the sandblasted Blenko label, it can be dated to 1959 or 1960. Although many pieces bear this signature, collectors are willing—even eager—to pay a premium for them. Any marked item will therefore fall beyond the high end of the range. Needless to say, the designer's signature will also increase the value. If it is on an experimental piece that was not put into production, it will be "priceless" or worth whatever someone is willing to pay.

Desirability and subsequent higher price will also be determined by quality of design and craftsmanship. Generally, the earlier objects were made by the most skillful blowers, and even the thickness of the glass differs. Seed glass with tiny bubbles is often seen in earlier pieces. Anderson's designs—as long as they were made while he was designing them—generally show the best quality blowing. Good design is a more subjective call, but the three designers of the period each made many good designs—and some not-so-good designs. Size probably affects Blenko prices the most. Affectionately nicknamed "big ass Blenko," these extreme pieces, introduced by Husted, are among the rarest, most desirable, and priciest.

In addition to the above criteria, color can also affect value. Rosé, made in 1963 and 1964, is both rare and sought-after. A Rosé piece would be at the high end of the range—if not higher. Charcoal, another uncommon color, also commands a slightly higher price. Chestnut, Chartreuse, Surf Green, Pine Green, and Plum are atypical Blenko colors that do not necessarily fetch a higher price, and Crystal can lower it. Subdued Honey and Olive Green are usually at the low end of the color value range. Clear pastels like Sea Green and Sky Blue would fall in the middle. Intense spectrum colors—Ruby, Persian, Amethyst, Jonquil—might be at the high end. The two most popular and frequently-found colors—Turquoise (Blenko blue) and Tangerine (amberina) are also among the most desirable.

Finish—plain or crackle—should not affect value. Crackle is achieved by placing the hot glass object into cold water—the temperature change causes it to crack.

William H. Blenko Sr.

After it is put back into the glory hole to seal the cracks, it is placed into the mold to regain its shape. Many Blenko collectors prefer a plain finish, while many crackle glass collectors will pass up a piece of Blenko, unless it is crackled. Since these are personal preferences, they do not affect the market value of a piece, even if some would like us to believe otherwise.

With so many variables acting on pricing, you can expect to find pieces outside of the listed ranges. With growing activity in the market for fifties and sixties Blenko, some of the suggested ranges are certain to become outdated—soon. In any case, the coolest Blenko pieces will fetch the highest prices. Although *neither the author nor the publisher is responsible for any outcomes from consulting the prices in this guide,* we do hope that they are of some value when buying or selling Blenko glass.

The purpose of this book is to introduce the designs and the designers who brought this American company at "Milton on the Mud" to the attention of modern glass enthusiasts. It is to persuade the readers (some may not need persuading) that Blenko's cool American fifties and sixties glass warrants inclusion in the history of twentieth-century design as well as in both private and public collections. The company is aware of the importance of its own history, and the Blenko Visitor Center houses a mini-museum displaying examples of its past designs. Museums like the Huntington Museum of Art have also recognized the quality of Blenko's design, and their collection and displays of it are impressive. The drive to the Huntington is as unique as the building. Spiraling up a hill on a narrow tree-line road speckled with filtered sunlight and shadows makes the approach feel almost like a ride in a theme park, and the museum—the little gem at the top—makes the effort worthwhile.

One display worth noting was the exhibit held in fall of 1999 which recognized Winslow Anderson and his contribution to the company and to modern design. Besides Blenko's collection, many of the items in this volume were photographed at the Huntington Museum of Art in Huntington, West Virginia, after Anderson dug out his own pieces he had stashed away. As Blenko's first design director and one of three major contributors to a definition of cool fifties and sixties glass, it is appropriate that Anderson was chosen for the special exhibit at the close of the millennium. Before introducing Anderson and his work, the reader is invited to travel back in time with a visual sample of moments in Blenko's history.

Top: William H. Blenko Jr. signing glass.

Bottom: Lee Kennedy, Eddie Rubel, and Bob Stein.

Top: William H. Blenko Jr.

Bottom: Retailing Blenko.

# Chronology

**1854** William John Blenko born in London, England.

**1893** Blenko goes to America, arrives in Kokomo, Indiana, and begins making stained glass; finds himself in the midst of an economic depression with 20% unemployment and no churches to use his stained glass.

**1897** William Henry Blenko is born in Kokomo.

**1903** After the Kokomo factory fails, Blenko returns to England with his family.

**1909** Tries again in America, this time in Point Marion, Pennsylvania.

**1911** After another failure, Blenko begins making glass in Clarksburg, West Virginia.

**1913** Blenko gives up.

**1920** William Henry Blenko marries Marian Hunt, daughter of a Pittsburgh glass designer.

**1921** Blenko recovers from past failures and begins in Milton, West Virginia. He calls the company Eureka Art Glass Co., because he discovered the valuable formula for ruby glass and shouted, "eureka, I found it!"

**1922** Blenko's son William Henry (Bill) joins his glass business.

**1929** Experiments making decorative tableware for Carbones of Boston.

**1930s** No market for stained glass during the Depression, so Bill Blenko begins to focus on tableware. He hires Swedish glassmakers from the Huntington Tumbler Co., Axil (glassblower) and Louis (finisher) Muller to teach workers how to make quality table and decorative ware for Blenko.

**1932** Macy's in New York begins to carry Blenko tableware.

**1933** William John Blenko dies, leaving Bill as president; Blenko glass is featured at the "Century of Progress" Chicago World's Fair.

Top: Earl Carpenter demonstrating his craft.

Center: The factory.

Bottom: Color samples of sheet glass. *Courtesy of Blenko.*

Top: Behind the scene at the glass factory.

Bottom: Gathering the hot glass.

**1936** Colonial Williamsburg contracts Blenko to make their glass reproductions.

**late 1930s** Carl Ebert Erickson (1899-1966) works at Blenko; he and his brother head Erickson Glassworks in Bremen, Ohio, 1943-1961.

**early 1940s** World War II, forty-one glassworkers drafted, Bill Blenko is a captain in the Air Corps, production halted.

**1946** New factory built, booming postwar economy creates new demand for both stained glass and tableware.

**1946** Winslow Anderson begins as the first design director and elevates the level of artistic achievement.

**1952** Wayne Husted begins as the second design director and introduces oversized stoppered bottles and other fifties icons.

Group of Colonial Williamsburg reproductions (1936-1966). *Courtesy of Blenko.*

Williamsburg Restoration label.

Williamsburg pieces in Turquoise. *Courtesy of Blenko.*

Williamsburg teal finger bowl, after an English wine rinse.

Glassblower label

Early Blenko Handcraft foil label, used until c. 1982.

*Foil store display label.*
Courtesy of Blenko.

Cardboard model of new label.
*Courtesy of Blenko.*

New cellophane label.

**1958** Sandblast signature created by Husted.

**1959** First all color catalog created by Husted.

**1960s** Glass artists and members of the new studio glass movement come to Blenko to learn.

**1961** Sandblasted signature phased out.

**1963** Joel Myers begins as design director and also learns to blow glass.

**1966** Blenko Visitors' Center opens; Colonial Williamsburg reproductions discontinued.

**1969** Bill Blenko dies, leaving his son, William Henry Jr., as president; many West Virginia glass companies are forced to close because of foreign competition and increased production costs.

**1970** John Nickerson begins as design director.

**1975** Don Shepherd begins as design director.

**1980** West Virginia Annual Birthday Piece.

**1987** Publication of *Blenko Glass 1930-1953*.

**1988** Hank Adams begins as design director.

**1994** Chris Gibbons begins as design director.

**1995** Matthew Carter begins as design director.

**1996** William Blenko steps down, and Richard Deakin Blenko becomes president.

**1998** Documentary on Blenko's history *Hearts of Glass* aired on public television.

**1999** Huntington Museum of Art holds special exhibit to honor Blenko and its first design director, Winslow Anderson.

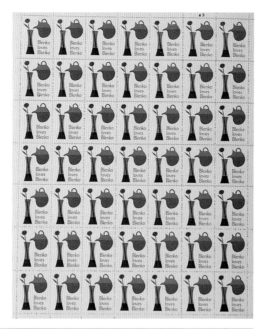

"Blenko Loves Blenko" stamps. Made as a sales promotion and used only in 1960 and 1961—Blenko glass loves to be with other Blenko glass.

*House & Gardens* December 1966 advertisement illustrating "Blenko loves Blenko."

*House & Gardens* December 1969 advertisement illustrating "Blenko loves Blenko."

# BLENKO COLORS 1947-1971

Color can influence prices because of rarity and/or desirability. Crystal is usually the least desirable "color." Tangerine and Turquoise are desirable but common. Rosé, produced only in 1963 and 1964 is rare and desir- able. Other rare colors include Mulberry, Lilac, Juniper, Plum, and Lime, so examples will usually sell at the high end of the range or as much as double the "normal" market value.

| | |
|---|---|
| 1947 | Amethyst, Marine Crystal, Ruby, Sea Green, Sky Blue, Turquoise |
| 1948 | Honey, Marine Crystal, Ruby, Sea Green, Sky Blue, Turquoise |
| 1949 | Amethyst, Marine crystal, Ruby, Sea Green, Sky Blue, Turquoise |
| 1950 | Amethyst, Marine Crystal, Ruby, Sea Green, Sky Blue, Turquoise |
| 1951 | Amber, Amethyst, Chartreuse, Emerald, Ice Blue, Marine Crystal, Sea Green, Turquoise |
| 1952 | Amber, Amethyst, Chartreuse, Crystal, Emerald, Ice Blue, Lime, Sea Green |
| 1953 | Amber, Amethyst, Chartreuse, Crystal, Emerald, Ice Blue, Lime, Sea Green |
| 1954 | Amber, Amethyst, Charcoal, Chartreuse, Crystal, Lime, Sea Green, Teal |
| 1955 | Amber, Amethyst, Charcoal, Chartreuse, Crystal, Lime, Sea Green, Teal |
| 1956 | Amber, Amethyst, Charcoal, Crystal, Gold, Lime, Sea Green, Teal |
| 1957 | Amethyst, Charcoal, Crystal, Gold, Juniper, Sea Green, Tangerine, Teal |
| 1958 | Charcoal, Crystal, Gold, Jade, Mulberry, Sea Green, Tangerine, Teal |
| 1959 | Aqua, Crystal, Jonquil, Lilac, Nile, Persian, Tangerine, Turquoise |
| 1960 | Crystal, Jonquil, Lilac, Persian, Raindrop (Crystal), Regal (Ruby), Rialto (White Opalescent Crystal with Ruby trim), Sea Green, Tangerine, Turquoise |
| 1961 | Amethyst, Charcoal, Crystal, Jonquil, Persian, Regal, Sea Green, Tangerine, Turquoise |
| 1962 | Amethyst, Charcoal, Crystal, Jonquil, Sea Green, Tangerine, Turquoise |
| 1963 | Crystal, Jonquil, Rosé, Sea Green, Tangerine, Turquoise |
| 1964 | Crystal, Olive Green, Jonquil, Rosé, Sea Green, Tangerine, Turquoise |
| 1965 | Chestnut, Crystal, Honey, Olive Green, Peacock, Tangerine, Turquoise |
| 1966 | Crystal, Honey, Olive Green, Peacock, Tangerine, Turquoise |
| 1967 | Crystal, Honey, Olive Green, Plum, Tangerine, Turquoise |
| 1968 | Crystal, Honey, Lemon, Olive Green, Tangerine, Turquoise |
| 1969 | Crystal, Lemon, Olive Green, Tangerine, Turquoise, Wheat |
| 1970 | Crystal, Olive Green, Surf Green, Tangerine, Turquoise, Wheat |
| 1971 | Charcoal, Crystal, Olive Green, Tangerine, Turquoise, Wheat |

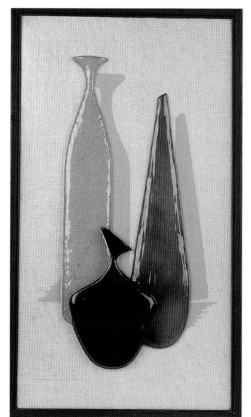 

Fifties wall plaques with iconic modern glass inspired by Blenko.

Transparent color and form—Blenko loves Blenko. Sea Green and Rose.

Juxtaposed color and form. Persian and Olive.

14

Top left: Construction of the Visitor Center.

Top right: Blenko Visitor Center opens in 1966.

Bottom left: Flyer for Visitor Center and factory outlet in Milton.

Right: Richard Blenko at the Visitor Center.

Above: Display of Blue Top Mountain Glass in 1977.

Top right: Shepherd's etched presentation piece for Governor Moore.
*Courtesy of Blenko.*

Right: Shepherd's "Kentucky Wild Cat" etched on cobalt vase.
*Courtesy of Blenko.*

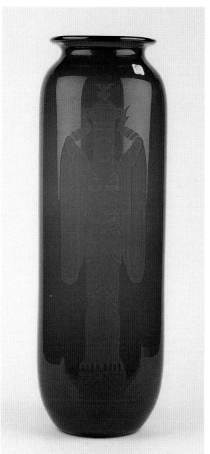

7527
6½" dia.
$10.00
Made in
tangerine only

7529
9½" high
$15.00

7528
7½" high
$15.00

7525
7½" high
$10.00

COLORS AS SHOWN ONLY

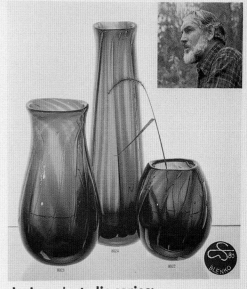

**designer's studio series:** is a group of vases in three shapes created by BLENKO's designer, Don Shepherd. Every piece is made offhand and is unique. The monogram signature of Don Shepherd along with the year (80) and the company name (BLENKO) are signed on the bottom of every vase and a personalized name tag will be shipped with each piece of glass.

Don Shepherd has been design director for the Blenko Glass Company since the fall of 1975. Not only is he recognized as a glass designer and artist, but he is also well known for his work in architectural arts and environmental design. He is an exhibitor in the current exhibition, "New Glass—a Worldwide Survey".

Top left: Special cobalt vase with spectacular etched design. *Courtesy of Blenko.*

Top right: Detail.

Bottom left: Shepherd's Designer Studio Series for 1980.

Bottom right: Unusual two-color swirl pieces for 1975 (similar to the Charisma line of 1972).

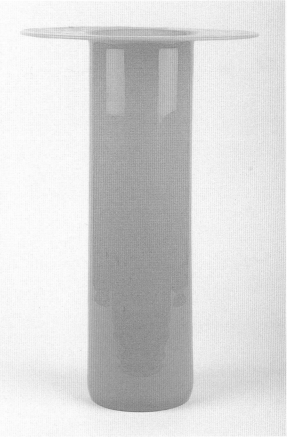

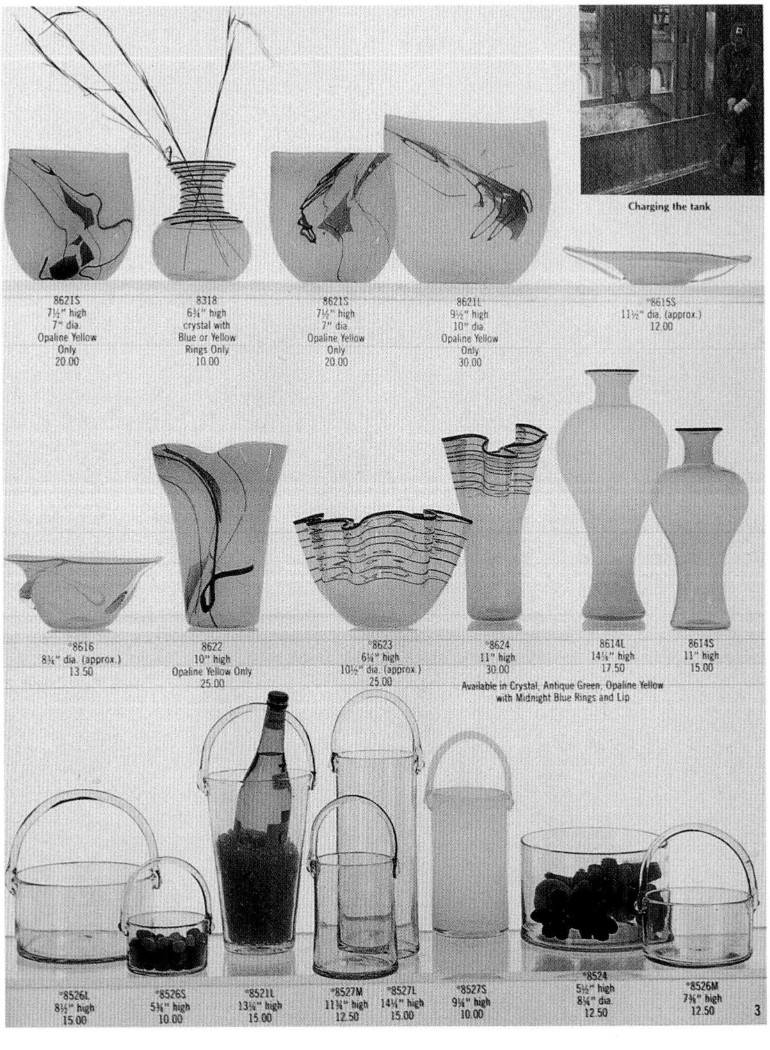

Top left: Face vase by Shepherd. *Courtesy of Blenko.*

Top right: #8319 cylinder vase by Shepherd. *Courtesy of Blenko.*

Left: Opaline Yellow in 1986 catalog, by Shepherd.

Charging the tank

| 8621S | 8318 | 8621S | 8621L | *8615S |
|---|---|---|---|---|
| 7½" high | 6¾" high | 7½" high | 9½" high | 11½" dia. (approx.) |
| 7" dia. | crystal with | 7" dia. | 10" dia. | 12.00 |
| Opaline Yellow | Blue or Yellow | Opaline Yellow | Opaline Yellow | |
| Only | Rings Only | Only | Only | |
| 20.00 | 10.00 | 20.00 | 30.00 | |

| *8616 | 8622 | *8623 | *8624 | 8614L | 8614S |
|---|---|---|---|---|---|
| 8¼" dia. (approx.) | 10" high | 6¼" high | 11" high | 14¼" high | 11" high |
| 13.50 | Opaline Yellow Only | 10½" dia. (approx.) | 30.00 | 17.50 | 15.00 |
| | 25.00 | 25.00 | | | |

Available in Crystal, Antique Green, Opaline Yellow with Midnight Blue Rings and Lip

| *8526L | *8526S | *8521L | *8527M | *8527L | *8527S | *8524 | *8526M |
|---|---|---|---|---|---|---|---|
| 8¼" high | 5⅜" high | 13¼" high | 11¼" high | 14¼" high | 9¼" high | 5½" high | 7⅜" high |
| 15.00 | 10.00 | 15.00 | 12.50 | 15.00 | 10.00 | 8¼" dia. | 12.50 |
| | | | | | | 12.50 | |

3

Opposite page: Other odd stoppers without ground area that fits into the bottle.

18

| 9229M | 9229L | 9229S |
|---|---|---|
| 19¾" high | 25¾" high | 16½" high |
| 35.00 | 42.00 | 30.00 |
| N/A in Emerald, Cobalt, Amethyst or Topaz | | |

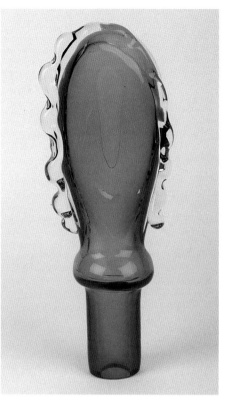

#9104-L 23-inch vase by Hank Adams.
*Courtesy of Patricia Attenson.*

#9229-M-L-S vase by Adams.

Imperfect stopper for 9229 vase.

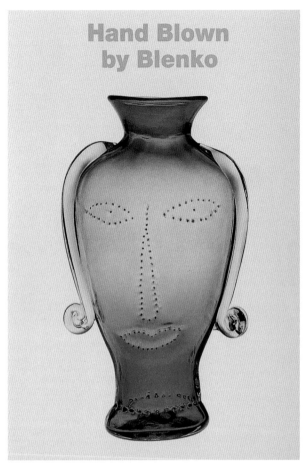

## Hand Blown
## by Blenko

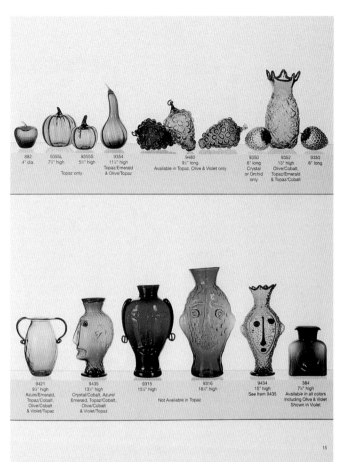

# Blenko Glass USA

## Millennium Vase

Only 2,000 of these magnificent vases will be created to celebrate the new millennium. Designed by Blenko designer Matt Carter, each vase will be individually numbered. Be one of the first and few to retain one of these elegant millennium vases.

Item # "2000"    Available in Emerald, Kiwi, Crystal & Cobalt    $30.00
                 (See order form)

Contact: Blenko Glass Company, Inc.
P.O. Box 67
Fairgrounds Road
Milton, WV 25541
304-743-9081   Fax: 304-743-0547
E-mail: Blenko@usa.net
Internet: http://www.Blenkoglass.com

Top left: #931-S face vase by Adams.

Top right: Fruit and faces in 1994 catalog.

Bottom left: Advertisement for Millennium Vase by Matt Carter.

Bottom right: Ebony line by Carter for 1999.

Matt Carter, William Blenko Jr., and Wayne Husted looking at *Metropolis* outside with the piles of cullet.

In the summer of 1999 Wayne Husted and Matt Carter dug up the old mold for the 633 bowl and made this Crystal and Cobalt monstrosity for the author (and she loves it).

Signatures.

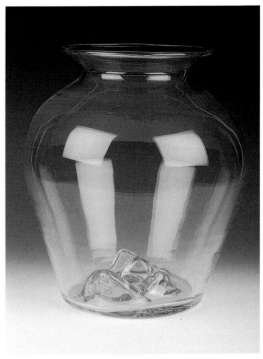

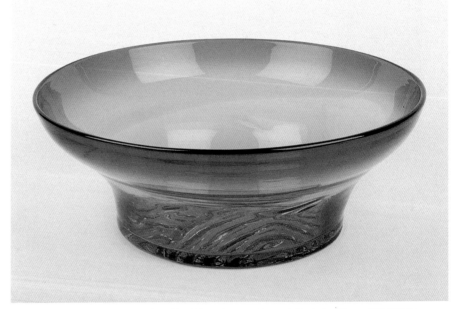

Top left: 1980 West Virginia Annual Birthday Piece (WVABP) by Don Shepherd. *Courtesy of Blenko.*

Top right: 1981 Annual Birthday Piece (WVABP) by Don Shepherd, Crystal vase with mountains. *Courtesy of Blenko.*

Bottom left: 1982 WVABP by Shepherd, Crystal bowl with mountains and Cobalt crackle rim. *Courtesy of Blenko.*

Bottom right: 1983 WVABP by Shepherd, 13-inch two-tone bowl with textured bottom. *Courtesy of Blenko.*

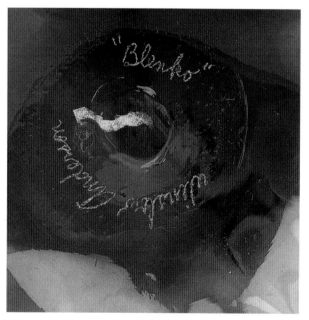

Top left: Pitcher with pinched spout, in emerald green. *Courtesy of Winslow Anderson.*

Top center: One-of-a-kind Sea Green bulbous vase with long neck and flared opening, designed by Anderson in the late 1940s. *Courtesy of Winslow Anderson.*

Top right: Emerald green epergne, designed by Anderson but possibly not produced. *Courtesy of Winslow Anderson.*

Bottom left: Green flat-bottomed bowl with three legs, inspired by archaic Chinese bronze form, an experimental piece by Anderson, since only those with round bowls were produced. *Courtesy of Winslow Anderson.*

Bottom right: Anderson's signature, sometimes found on his designs.

The Huntington Museum of Art Board of Trustees
cordially invites you to the opening of

# Winslow Anderson
## *Artist / Designer*
### August 22, 1999 - January 9, 2000

Meet the artist during a reception on
Saturday, August 21, 1999
7 p.m. to 9 p.m.

Please RSVP by Monday, August 16, 1999
304•529•2701

Invitation to the Huntington Museum of Art's special Anderson
exhibit. *From Eason Eige, photo Courtesy of the Huntington.*

# Chapter 2
# Wayne Husted

Wayne Husted with his Blenko designs, early 1950s. *Courtesy of Wayne Husted.*

...I was told that the principal New York agent was so negative toward Chartreuse (a new color Winslow Anderson had selected) that he promised he wouldn't have one piece of glass in that "frog shit color" in his showrooms. Bill Blenko Sr., in typical fashion, reminded the agent that he was not the designer. The color was produced and was an instant and long-running success on the market.

—*Wayne Husted*

*The following is excerpted from (slightly edited) e-mails sent by Husted.*

I was born in Hudson, New York, in 1927. My father was a Methodist minister—very energetic and academic, but also very artistic. He played the piano and included entertainment with his sermons by drawing pictures, referring to his illustrated one-man shows as his "chalk talks." There were four siblings, and we never owned a house. Instead, we moved from one church-owned parsonage to another every two or three years. When I wound up designing for Blenko, I usually communicated with the glass blowers by drawing the shapes I wanted them to make in chalk on the glass factory floor. I now wonder if this was learned or genetic—frankly, I suspect the latter.

I graduated from Hudson High School in June 1945, near the end of World War II. My teachers had considered me a somewhat troublesome pupil, always wanting to draw in class and ignoring their lectures. I was sent to the principal's office more than once with a note typically reading, "Wayne Husted would rather draw than study his [Algebra], so I am expelling him from my class room."

After graduating I immediately joined the U.S. Coast Guard, and while still in training on Long Island, the Japanese surrendered. Although I had already passed the exams for officer's training, I opted instead to leave the service to attend regular college. (Before my discharge, I had the honor of leading a six-man honor guard for Admiral Nimitz's car through the victory parade up Fifth Avenue in New York in August of 1945. So every time I see the famous pictures of the VJ day celebrations in Times Square, I try to find me in the crowd of sailors.)

My family decided that I was the "chosen" of the siblings to follow my father and become a "preacher," but since I personally did not "feel the calling," I enrolled in a pre-med course at Mohawk College in Utica, New York. After one year, and taking night courses in painting and sculpture, I transferred to Geneva College in Beaver Falls, Pennsylvania. While on summer vacation, quite accidentally, a high school guidance counselor led me to Alfred University. But the design department only accepted about forty new freshmen out of about 1,500 applications. Undaunted by those odds, and with his usual dynamism, my father gathered up a portfolio of my work and drove eight hours for a meeting with Charles Harder, the great and wonderful head of Alfred's Ceramic Design Department. The fortunate coincidence turned out to be that Alfred actually preferred students without prior formal art training—they had their own ideas about teaching art and design and did not want the added burden of having their students un-learn whatever they had already been taught about art.

The next five years (1947-1952) were spent at Alfred. It was a seminal time for the university—the generation of classes behind me had spawned the likes of Winslow Ander son and Glidden Parker. And Alfred was an interesting surrogate for a religious career, teaching that design is a statement of philosophy. They "preached" the Bauhaus morality about honesty to materials and social responsibility. I graduated with a double undergraduate degree—B.A in English and B.F.A. in Industrial Ceramic Design, followed by an M.F.A. in Industrial Ceramic Design.

## Blenko

So what were the ten years at Blenko like? When I returned last month [June 1999] I had not been back to "Milton on the Mud" for thirty-six years. I had been chosen by no less than Charles Harder himself to be the new "padre" in a remote town. Armed with advice from Harder, "Don't accept less than $5,200 per year," and from Winslow Anderson, "The people here are great, the opportunity is great, but you will feel very isolated," I was ready.

I began on April Fool's Day, 1952. Within a few minutes of meeting William Blenko Sr., I told him that I had no experience with glass. His response, typical of his personality, was, "Great! Then you'll try things you wouldn't try if you knew something about glass." He had a way of winning respect and loyalty. If he had a flaw it was that he was tight with a dollar. I cannot make a negative judgment about that flaw after all these years, because who knows how careful he had to be with money in order to keep Blenko alive and make it grow as he did?

In one respect, my experience with the glass workers was not unlike joining a college fraternity. Glass workers (and not limited to West Virginia), like frat boys, like to test the mettle of any newcomer. Although I arrived with my wife, they invited me to join them alone under the Mud River bridge. This is where they kept six or seven gallons of white lightning in jars on ropes (long before "Soap-on-a-Rope"). They sold from this creative "point of purchase" as well. I felt it was my duty to oblige with several long draws on the jug, but the consequences were indeed a night to remember (or forget).

Each year for ten years, I came up with fifty to sixty designs in time for the annual sales meeting in November. All of the Blenko sales agents assembled to accept or reject the designs that were submitted—a ritual established before I arrived at Blenko, and I believe one that is still followed today. There was frequent disagreement between the salesmen, but inevitably, the only designs rejected by

Husted and glassworker examining the product. *Courtesy of Wayne Husted.*

Bill Blenko were rejected not because of design, but because they could not be made profitably, and these were few in number. One of the greatest things about Blenko was its "listen to the designer" policy. When I submitted my first line for 1953 to the representatives, the same salesman with the "frog shit" opinion complained that the stopper in one of my decanters was too tall. Bill Blenko reminded him that he was not a designer, and furthermore, if a designer made one bad judgment, his batting average would still surpass the salesman's. It was this kind of leadership that bred loyalty to William Blenko Sr.

On the negative side, Milton and Blenko were an isolated fiefdom. I soon learned that the Blenko family were not unlike royalty in the "kingdom" of Milton, West Virginia. The locals privately kidded about "Prince William the second" and "Queen Marion."

I loved making new shapes in glass and experimenting with processes. One of my designs even won an award in the Corning Museum competition and was featured in *Glass 1959*. Perhaps what I was best known for were those huge bottles and decanters that came to typify the glass of that period. What I am not known for were the catalogs, but from 1953-1963 I took all of the photos, set up every shot, and did the layouts. In 1959 Blenko issued its first all-color catalog, and to eliminate the greenish edge on the glass shelving, I designed the special thick acrylic shelf system that is still being used forty-six years later!

I remained at Blenko until January 1963 after designing the 1963 line. From there I took a position as Director of Design and Product Development for Lancaster Colony, where I stayed for another ten years, until June of 1973. During that time I created new product designs for most of their sixteen divisions, including Indiana Glass and Colony Glass, plus products from rubber and plastic automobile accessories to plastic kitchen and bath items. Also during that time, I designed items for Viking Glass, such as their "Cabbage Bowls," which sold for over thirty-five years, and the "Lotus Bowls," made until Viking closed its furnace. Then I moved to Tiburon, California, a suburb across the bay from San Francisco, and designed for Vincent Lippe Company for ten years. This was followed by, yes, another ten years—this time with Anchor Hocking. After "retiring" from company work, I began my latest career as a freelance designer.

Husted's experimental "Swedish" designs made at Blenko. *Courtesy of Wayne Husted.*

Left: Husted drawing for form handle pitcher.

Center: Drawing for famous #5427 "Gurgle" bottle.

Right: Drawing for #6218 sun face decanter.

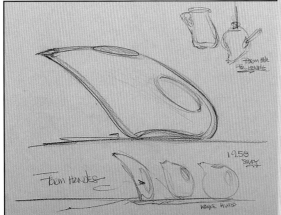

Turquoise decanters:
#587-S Spool, h. 15-1/2" $400-500
#5823 Spouted, h. 16". $400-500
#5427-S $200-275. *Photo courtesy of Gordon Harrell.*

Turquoise decanters and pitchers:
#5729, $300-500
#572 Tall Spouted, h. 21". $600-800
#571 Ice Tea, h. 15" $400-500. *Photo courtesy of Gordon Harrell.*

Drawing for #552 Portrait Vase

Drawing for #564 Decanter

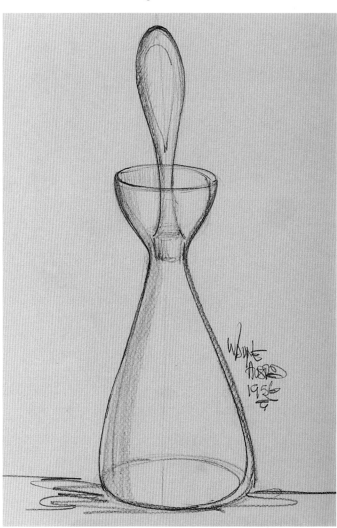

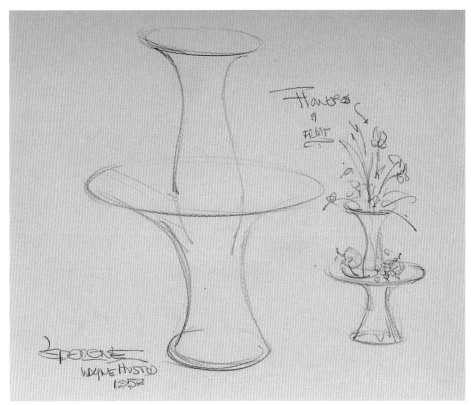

Drawing for #5833 Epergne

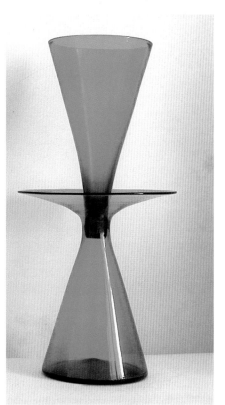

#5833 epergne in Turquoise, h. 19".
*Photo courtesy of Gordon Harrell.*
$650-850

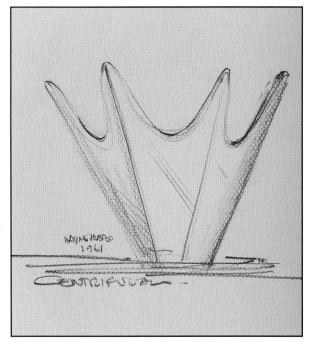

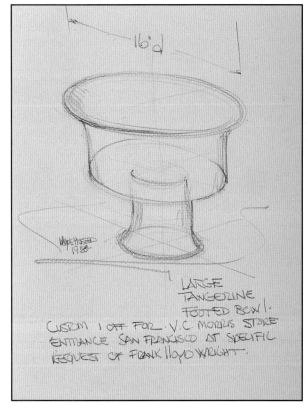

Top: Drawing for #6141 bowl.

Bottom: Drawing for large Tangerine footed bowl, custom made in 1953 for V.C. Morris store entrance in San Francisco, at the request of Frank Lloyd Wright.

Top: Drawing for ship's decanter.

Bottom: Drawing for Charcoal jar with Crystal faces.

#5720 "Napoleon Decanter" with #5717 tall vase.　　　#6222 and #6223 textured vases.

Experimental three-lobed bowl in Turquoise, Nile, and Ruby with sandblasted signature, c. 1960. $150-250. *Courtesy of Carol Seman.*

Gold #5728 covered jar, $600-800
#582 large goblet, h. 15" $250-300
#5826-M decanter, h. 20" $200-300
#920-L decanter, h. 22" $125-175.
*Photo courtesy of Gordon Harrell.*

# Chapter 3
# Joel Philip Myers

Joel Myers, the first hands-on designer, at Blenko, c. 1966.
*Courtesy of Joel Myers.*

My approach to glass is to allow the material an expression of its own. Press the material to the utmost, and it will suggest ideas and creative avenues to the responsive artist.

*—Joel Myers, 1964*

Joel Philip Myers was born in Peterson, New Jersey, in 1934. From 1951 to 1954 he studied at Parsons School of Design and graduated with honors in the Department of Advertising Design. He then worked as a package designer for Donald Deskey Assoc. Industrial Design Consultants in New York. Myers interrupted his commercial design career to study ceramic design with Richard Kjaergaard in Copenhagen, Denmark, from 1957 to 1958, and also took a summer job with an industrial design firm in Copenhagen. He returned to the States and worked as a package-graphic designer for two industrial design consulting firms in New York. Then from 1960 to 1963 he studied ceramic design at New York State College of Ceramics at Alfred University, where he earned B.F.A. and M.F.A. degrees.

Like his predecessors, Anderson and Husted, Myers was hired by Blenko Glass without training in either glass design or crafting. But as Director of Design from 1963 to 1970, Myers learned on the job much of what he would need to eventually become a proficient artist-designer in glass. And many of his designs for Blenko are among the most sought after by collectors today. His exaggerated tall slender bottles, his series with airtwist inclusions in paperweight stoppers, his vessels with applied spirals, and his creative use of molded decoration are but a few of his cool sixties designs that came to exemplify Blenko in particular and modern handmade production glass in general. But

unlike Anderson and Husted, who went on to enjoy successful careers as industrial designers, Myers became one of the pioneers of the studio glass movement. As Husted astutely observed: "The studio glass that has robbed Blenko of much of the "art" glass market is much more intricate in composition with rods and canes and combinations of many more elements that mount up to symphonies...while Blenko is mired in a commercial line with a few notes and chords, no matter how beautiful the individual chords may be." Myers could do both.

This versatility, his ability to coax the material, to bring out the best it could offer, made Myers both one of Blenko's cool sixties designers and an internationally recognized studio artist. And while he worked to perfect this studio art, he also taught others as Professor of Art at Illinois State University in Normal, Illinois, from 1970 to 1997. Not surprisingly, he founded its Glass Department. For his last two years, from 1997 to 1999, he held the distinguished title of Professor Emeritus. The lists of honors, fellowships, awards, publications, exhibitions, and museum collections fills a 17-page resume—and these are just in list form. His glass has been shown in more than eighty-five exhibits around the world since 1975; he has had nearly sixty one-man exhibits in the United States, Canada, and Europe; his work is represented in the collections of more than seventy museums worldwide. Highlights include his participation as panelist and demonstrator at the International Glass Symposium in Zurich, Switzerland, in 1972; he was on the board of directors of the Glass Art Society from 1974-78 and 1982-86 and president from 1975-76; the National Endowment for the Arts awarded him Craftsman Fellowships from 1976-77 and 1984; and the American Crafts

Council made him a Fellow in 1980; in 1993, his one-man exhibit traveled from Denmark to Germany and Switzerland.

Myers has come a long way since Blenko, and yet his production designs from that period are in many respects no less worthy of recognition than his sophisticated one-of-a-kind work.

For his thirty year (1969-1999) retrospective exhibit held at Barry Friedman Ltd. in New York, the brochure featured quotes by noted author Dan Klein and Associate Editor of *Art in America,* Janet Koplos:

> Like Matisse, Klee and Nolde...Joel Philip Myers is a superb colorist. He uses color to dazzle and delight with. He creates a deeply personal sense of beauty with his landscape collages and there is a rhythm and movement to his work that makes one feel that it might suddenly spring to life...It is this living feeling that makes Joel Philip Myers' glass so special...It has been a relationship that has enriched the recent history of decorative arts and left him one of the most important and original protago-

Myers working, c. 1990. *Courtesy of Joel Myers.*

nists in the story of that twentieth-century phenomenon called "New Glass."
—*Dan Klein*

> His is one of the few bodies of work in glass that can be compared with painting and not fall short...His abstraction, and his collage-like composition focus attention on the nuances of color and shape relationships—just as any abstract painting would—while taking advantage of the particular capabilities of his chosen material.
—*Janet Koplos*

Yet the qualities that have brought him praise for his studio work—color, movement, form, shape relationships, the ability to take advantage of the material and to dazzle—were already present in his work at Blenko.

The following collection of pieces and photos are courtesy of Joel Philip Myers.

#659-L cylinder vases with weighted bottoms, with experimental cylinder vases, 1964/65.

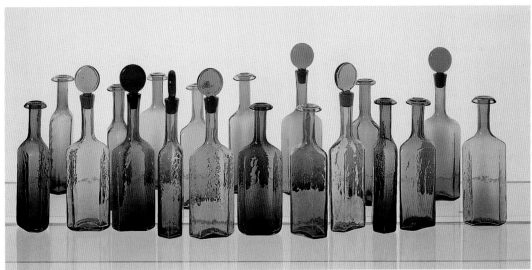

Top: Experimental dented vases, 1965.

Center: #6612 bottles and #6627 decanters.

Bottom: #6624 decanters.

Top left: Experimental decanter, 1964.

Center left: Experimental bottle with weighted bottom, c. 1964.

Bottom left: Experimental cylinder vases with flat collar, the 1964 inspiration for #8319 nearly two decades later.

Right: Special Blenko designer signed limited edition, in Muranese sommerso style, produced 1964-1966.

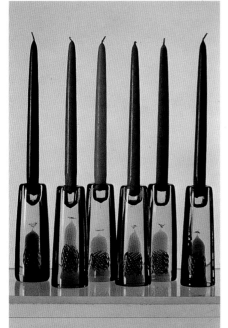

Top left: Form studies, 1966.

Top right: #6822 bottle without stopper, not produced.

Bottom left: #6824 paperweight candle holders, the cover of the 1968 catalog.

Bottom right: #6819 cool heavily textured bottle/decanters.

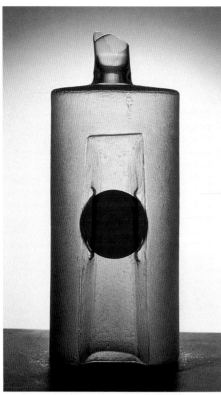

Left: Color Study #1, 1997; in 1999 exhibit "Joel Philip Myers: Dialogues, Enticements and Color Studies" at the Marx-Saunders Gallery, Ltd. in Chicago.

Right: "Enticement #2" 1998; exhibited 1999.

"Dialogue 6" 1998; also exhibited 1999.

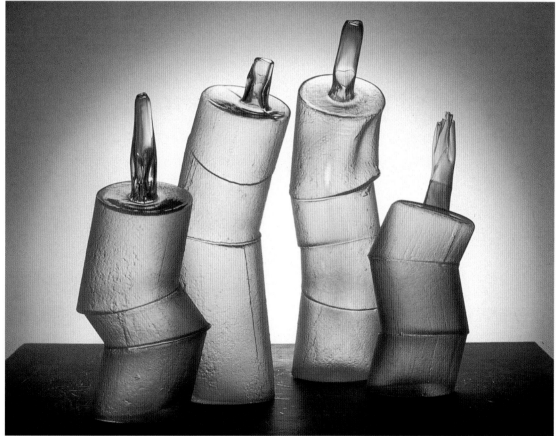

Top: "Dialogue #5" 1998; exhibited 1999.

Bottom: "Dialogue #8" 1998, tallest 13".

## Chapter 4
# Stoppers

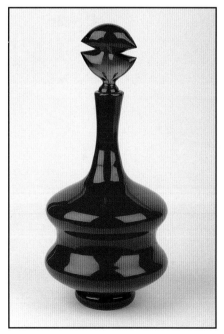 

Top left: #38 decanter (introduced 1938). One of Blenko's earliest decanters, in deep blue with long neck, flat collar, teardrop stopper and two-part base. *Courtesy of Blenko.* $100-125.

Bottom left: #5720 Napoleon Decanter. Husted 1957. Named by designer Wayne Husted because of the stopper resembling Napoleon's hat; shown in deep Tangerine. h. 15". *Courtesy of the Huntington.* $200-300.

Top right: #37 decanters (1937); *left,* 11-3/4" green decanter with teardrop stopper; phased out, leaving the popular flame stopper version (*right*) in the line for many years; shown in Tangerine (amberina). h. 13". $80-100; $50-60.

Bottom right: Husted's drawing of Napoleon Decanter.

#5921 Jonquil and #5823 Tangerine decanters with pulled appendages. $350-450, $400-500. *Photo courtesy of Gordon Harrell.*

#5419 Sea Green pinched decanter with crystal flame or claw stopper, h. 19-1/2" $400-500

#6838-TO decanter. Myers 1968, design 38. Turquoise ("Blenko blue") decanter with Olive Green spiral around neck. h. 15-3/4". *Courtesy of Blenko.* $100-125.

#6836-OT decanter. Myers 1968, design 36. Olive Green decanter with applied foot and Turquoise spiral. h. 13-3/4". *Courtesy of the Huntington.* $100-125.

#6836-CT decanter. Crystal with Tur-
quoise spiral. $100-125.

Detail of neck and stopper.

#445-D decanter. 1944, design 5. Crystal
crackle decanter with applied Turquoise
rosettes around the base and matching
stopper. h. 12". $90-110.

Advertisement in *House Beautiful*, October 1968 showing
several applied spiral variations. *Courtesy of Blenko.*

# BLENKO
## COLOR · CRAFTSMANSHIP · DESIGN

The ancient art of making handcraft glassware
can be observed in the Blenko Visitor Center.
Send name, address for descriptive color folder.

BLENKO GLASS COMPANY
MILTON, WEST VIRGINIA

AT BETTER STORES EVERYWHERE

#6822 and 6831-LT (Lemon with Tangerine trim) decanters. h. 18-1/4 and 23". $250-350 each. *Photo courtesy of Gordon Harrell.*

#588 Architectural decanter in Charcoal with crystal stopper. h. 30". $1400-1600. *Photo courtesy of Gordon Harrell.*

Left: #49 pinched decanter in Cobalt blue. *Courtesy of the Huntington.* $50-60.

Bent neck 948 decanter and #9485 oil/vinegar cruet, recipient of the Museum of Modern Art's "Good Design Award," classic (and widely copied) Anderson design in Sea Green and Amethyst with mushroom stopper; with another classic—the same decanter with straight neck and flame stopper. The bent version was created accidentally while making the straight decanter. h. 13" and 16". *Courtesy of Winslow Anderson.* $150-175, $75-100, $75-100.

Plum decanters:
#6631 with solid elongated stopper, h. 21-1/2" and #6529 h. 20".
$250-350 each ($400-500 each in Plum).
*Photo courtesy of Gordon Harrell.*

52

Top: #6122-L and #6122-S decanters. Husted 1961, design 22. Tangerine decanters with elongated flame stopper that is not ground and fits loosely in neck. h. 27" & 16-1/2". $250-300; $75-100.

Bottom: #6626-S. Myers 1966, design 26. Slender Tangerine decanter with solid conical stopper; shown with #6122-L with stopper out to show length. h. 16". $75-100.

#6530-S decanter. Myers, 1965, design 30. Honey optic decanter with squat base, long neck, and teardrop stopper. h. 14-1/4". $75-125.

#6516 decanters. Myers 1965, design 16. Tangerine decanters in crackle finish, with elaborate solid stoppers in two sizes. h. 14-1/2". $100-125 each.

#6516 in Olive Green crackle (colors often very similar). $100-125.

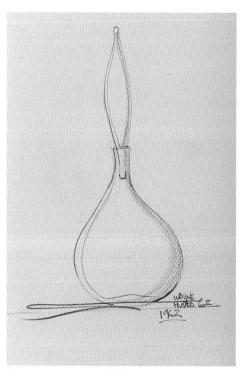

Husted drawing of #627 decanter.

#627-L decanters. Husted 1962, design 7. Tangerine and Honey crackle decanters showing variation in stopper height. Average h. 18". $100-125 each.

Decanters #6211-M, $200-300; #6316,
$800-1,000; and #6311-S, $200-300, in
Rosé, a special color made in 1963 & 1964
and very collectible.

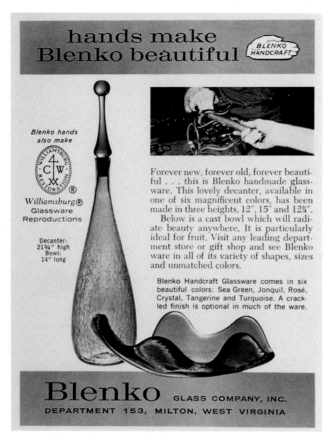

Blenko advertisement with #6311 decanter.

#6311-M decanter. Husted 1963, design 11. Tangerine decanter with unusual solid stopper that continues the form of the bottle. h. 15". $125-175.

Blenko advertisement with #6211.

#6211-M footed decanter. Husted 1962, design 11. Rosé footed decanter with large blown stopper repeating the form of the bottle. h. 15-3/4". $100-125; $200-300 Rosé.

Cover of 1963 catalog.

#5815-L and 588  30-in. Persian decanters with water-drop stoppers.
$400-600, $1200-1500
Photo courtesy of Gordon Harrell

#566 Heavy rectangular decanters with rounded shoulders and slightly serpentine base, in Tangerine and Amber. Each has interesting hand-blown irregularities—color change in Tangerine, stopper size, and slight tilt to Amber neck. h. 11". $125-175 each.

Left: #6212-S decanter. Husted 1962, design 12. Sea Green footed decanter with tall, slender, hollow, loose-fitting stopper. h. 16". $80-120.

Right: #6528-S & #6529 decanters. Myers 1965, designs 28 & 29. Large Honey (a 1965 color) decanters: *left* a slenderized version of Husted's earlier design; *right* with large "foot" integrated into the bottle form. h. 24" & 20". $125-150; $200-300.

#6942 & #646 decanters. Myers 1969, design 42 and 1964, design 6. Tangerine optic decanters: *left* with hollow round stopper and flat collar; *right* with long loose-fitting flame stopper. h. 11-2/4" & 17-1/2". $70-90; $75-100.

#6416 decanter in Rosé, a rare color, making the item more desirable. h. 14" $250-350 Rosé

#657-M decanters in Tangerine crackle and Peacock. $75-100 each.

Top: #5818 decanter with tumbler top in Sea Green. h. 14-1/2".
$125-175. *Photo courtesy of Gordon Harrell.*

Bottom left: #6627 & #565 decanters. Myers 1966, design 27;
Husted 1956, design 5. Tall cylindrical bottle-decanter in
Peacock, with earlier Sea Green wide-bottomed model. h. 17";
11". $90-110; $75-100.

Bottom center: #6728 decanter. Myers 1967, design 28. Plum
decanter with textured surface on both bottle and stopper. h. 16-3/4".
*Courtesy of the Huntington.* $125-150.

Bottom right: Blenko blue cylindrical decanter with textured bottle
and blown bubble stopper. *Courtesy of Blenko.* $65-85.

#6037 bubble decanter. Husted, 1960, design 37. Large Sea Green "bubble-wrap" decanter with overall bubble texture, large blown bubble stopper, sandblast signature, and "Blenko loves Blenko" sticker; shown with vases in the same series. h. 21-1/2". $200-250.

#6040 bubble decanter. Husted 1960, design 40. Shorter version of 6037 in Tangerine; with #715 small decanter. h. 15-1/2". $125-150.

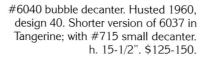

Tangerine decanters #5815-M and #5929-S. h. 24-1/2 and 22".
$250-300, $500-700. *Photo courtesy of Gordon Harrell.*

Turquoise decanters #5922L and #5929-S. h. 19-1/2 and 22-1/4".
$350-450, $500-700. *Photo courtesy of Gordon Harrell.*

#6310 decanters. Husted 1963, design 10. One of Husted's last unusual designs for Blenko before he left at the end of 1962; heavy Blenko blue and Tangerine bottles with five deeply molded bumps on one side and large hollow stopper. h. 14". $125-150 each.

#6310 in Blenko blue.

Italian copy of #6310 decanter with same overall dimensions but several differences: lighter weight, molded rather than ground bottom, no pontil, no ground stopper or inside neck to receive it, and only four bumps in the design. h. 14".

#6214 flask-decanter. Husted 1962, design 12. Sea Green flask-shaped decanter with abstract flower or sun ray texture, cast with an aluminum form designed by Husted. h. 11". *Courtesy of Mitchell Attenson.* $80-120.

Husted's drawing for 6214 flask-decanter.

Jonquil decanters:
#587-M, h. 23" $600-700
#6127, h. 26-1/2" $600-800
#5937, h. 23" $225-275. *Photo courtesy of Gordon Harrell.*

#649 decanters. Myers 1964, design 9. Tangerine smooth and Olive Green crackle bulbous decanters with blown stoppers of same shape as bottles. h. 13-1/4". $80-120 each.

Left: #654 decanters. Myers 1965, design 4. Tangerine and Blenko blue crackle decanters with elongated neck and solid bubble stopper. h. 12". $80-100 each.

Top right: #654 & 636-L decanters. Myers 1965, design 4; Husted 1963, design 6. Blenko blue crackle version of earlier design, with elongated neck and solid stopper; with Jonquil crackle with bubble stopper. h. 12"; 11". $80-100 each.

Bottom right: Myers decanter made only in 1964 for Gump's in California. h. 12-1/2". *Courtesy of Blenko.*

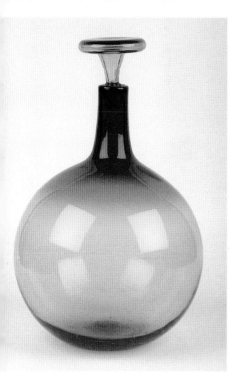

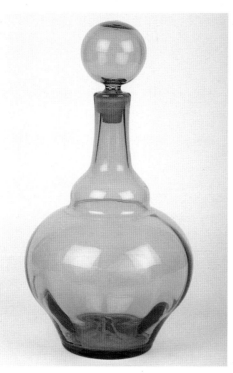

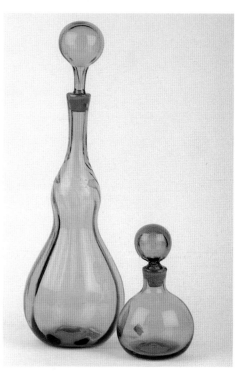

#648 decanter. Myers 1964, design 8. Large Tangerine bubble-shaped bottle with mushroom stopper. h. 19". *Courtesy of Mitchell Attenson.* $150-175.

#6935 decanter. Myers 1969, design 35. Two-part form with bubble stopper in wheat. h. 13-1/2". $70-90.

#6936 & #636-S decanters. Myers 1969, design 36; Husted 1963 (designed 1962), design 6. Olive Green with bubble stoppers, left with optic. h. 19"; 8". *Courtesy of Blenko.* $150-200; $45-55.

#638-L & #638-M decanters. Husted 1963, design 8. Jonquil pinched bottles with elongated necks and bubble stoppers, discontinued in 1964; shown with #561 decanter. h. 20" & 15". $125-175 ea.

#561 decanters. Husted 1956, design 1. Tall cone shaped decanters with elongated necks and mushroom stoppers in Tangerine and Jonquil. h. 22-1/2". $200-250 each.

#5815-M, #5815-S, & #5815-L decanters. Husted 1958, design 15. Turquoise, Persian, and Tangerine "genie bottles" with elongated necks and solid stoppers *(Courtesy of Mitchell Attenson)*; Persian, a 1959 color, with sandblast signature *(Courtesy of Ken Jupp)*. h. 24-1/2", 17", & 31". $200-275; $150-200 (+signature); $350-500.

Top left: Stopper.

Top right: Sandblasted signature.

Bottom: Husted sketch with decanter.

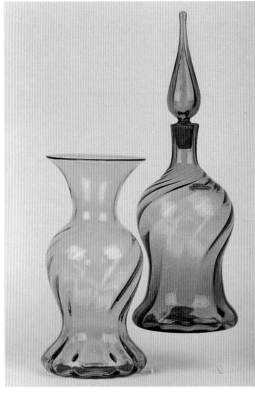

Left: #6954 decanter. Myers 1969, design 54. Large Wheat optic torso-shaped bottle with long neck and stopper. h. 27-1/4". $200-300.

Right: #6810 vase & #6811 decanter. Myers 1968, designs 10 & 11. Wheat spiral optic vase with pinched waist, and Honey optic decanter with flame stopper. h. 11" & 16-1/4". $50-70; $75-100.

Left: #587-L spool decanters in Jonquil and #5929-L in Tangerine. $1200-1600 each. *Photo courtesy of Gordon Harrell.*

Left: #6741 decanter. Myers 1967, design 41. Tall Honey decanter with airtwist paperweight stopper. h. 23-1/2". *Courtesy of Blenko.* $150-200.

Right: Detail.

#6716 decanter. Large squat Honey decanter with round airtwist paperweight stopper. h. 15". $150-225.

Left: #6724 bottle. Myers 1967, design 24. Tangerine bottle with heavy weighted base and flat collar. The Crystal airtwist paperweight stopper was used with other Tangerine pieces in this series. h. 14". $150-175.

Top right: #6716 in Tangerine, made only with Crystal stopper. $175-250.

Bottom right: Blenko advertisement in *House & Garden*, November 1967, showing paperweight and other elaborate stoppers. *Courtesy of Blenko*.

BLENKO 1972

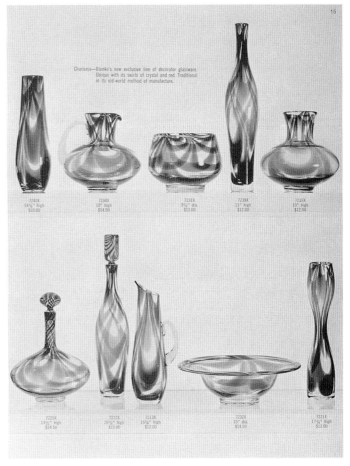

Top left: #7222-X Charisma bottle. John Nickerson, 1972, design 22. Tall, heavy bottle with red swirls in crystal and solid stopper, produced only in 1972, one of the rare instances where Blenko used internal rather than applied decoration. h. 21". $250-450. Charisma peaked at very high prices, but recent reproductions have had a negative influence on market values of originals.

Top right: Charisma stopper.

Bottom left: Front cover of Blenko 1972 catalog.

Bottom right: Charisma line in 1972 catalog.

#7222-X shown with #7239
Charisma bottle with red-orange
swirls, same height even though it
was made without a stopper.
$250-450 each.

Left: #5835 vase & #5825-L bottle. Husted 1958, designs 35 & 25. Twisted vase in Charcoal with tall twisted bottle and stopper in Jonquil. h. 11" & 23". *Courtesy of Blenko.* $60-80; $200-275.

Right: 5825-S in Tangerine. h. 19-1/2". $175-250.

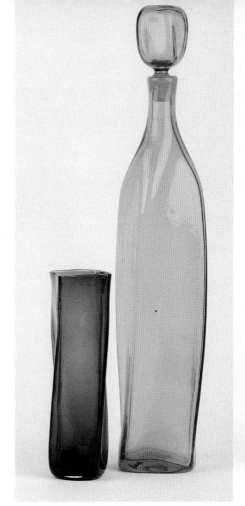

Blenko group in S & H Green Stamp book, c. 1960, with twist bottle, bubble-wrap vase, and others. *Courtesy of Blenko.*

*House Beautiful* cover with twist vase.

#6123-LL big bottle. Husted 1961, design 23.
One of Husted's "big ass Blenko" bottles in
Tangerine; shown with 64-B to show relative
size. h. 30". *Courtesy of William Emmerson.*
$600-800.

#5929-L giant decanter. Husted 1959, design 29. Huge Charcoal and
Ruby extreme design decanters, used to decorate Richard Blenko's
office. *Courtesy of Blenko.* $1,200-1,600 each.

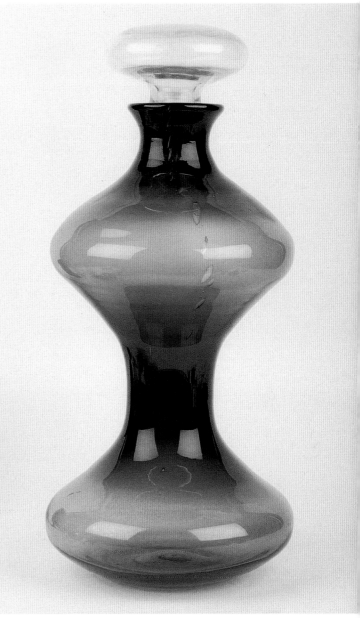

#5922-S decanters. Husted 1959, design 22. Curvilinear bottles and extreme stoppers, in Persian (solid version of stopper) and Tangerine (larger hollow version of stopper), both with sandblast signature. h. 14-1/2" & 15-1/2". $200-250 each (+signature).

#5719 Large Mushroom bottle. Husted 1957, design 19. Charcoal hourglass form bottle with crystal mushroom stopper. h. 20". *Courtesy of Blenko.* $350-450.

#6027 decanter. Husted 1960, design 27. Extreme design Lilac crackle decanter with pencil neck and shot glass stopper; a similar design by Fratelli Toso was pictured in the Corning Museum of Glass exhibit catalog. h. 17". *Courtesy of Myra Fortlage.* $200-250.

#6023 decanters in Olive Green and Tangerine, showing variation in height and in stopper design, both shown in catalogs. *Right: Courtesy of Mitchell Attenson.* $200-250 each.

Detail of stopper.

Detail of stopper.

Vintage photo of #6023 and other designs in front of the Blenko Visitor's Center. *Courtesy of Blenko.*

Left: #6944 decanter. Myers 1969, design 44. Honey decanter with large molded stopper. h. 9-1/2". $65-75.

Right: #6732-S Olive decanter and #6733 Turquoise vase. h.19-1/4 and 14-3/4". $300-350, $100-150. *Photo courtesy of Gordon Harrell.*

#708 decanter. Myers 1970, design 8. Variation of the earlier #6424 candle holder/vase, this Amberina decanter has slightly longer neck and stopper. h. 7-1/2". $45-55.

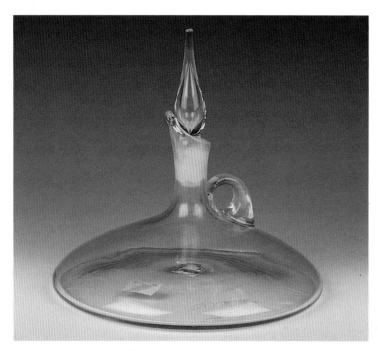

Crystal ship's decanter, a variant of #999, designed by Anderson, c. 1950. d. 10-3/4". *Courtesy of Winslow Anderson.*

#6819 textured decanter. Myers 1968, design 19. Crystal decanter with deep molded texture and ball stopper. h. 13-1/2". $100-150.

#6617 decanter. Myers 1966, design 17. Crystal decanter with textured flat sides and mushroom stopper. h. 10-1/4". $80-100.

# Chapter 5
# Vases

#64-A bottle/vases. Myers 1964. Emerald (1972), Amethyst, Turquoise, and Tangerine bottle-vases, each with a slightly different opening. Average h. 9". $35-45 each.

#64-A Plum, Emerald, Olive, Honey, Turquoise, and Tangerine example. $35-45 each.

#64-E & #64-A. Myers 1964. Green #64-E textured (with #64-B, the most common of the series) and Olive Green #64-A bottle-vases. h. 9". $25-35 each; (#64-B: $20-25).

#64-E in both Olive Green and Blenko blue. $25-35 each.

#64-D vases. Myers 1964. Honey and Blenko blue vases with optic and pronounced height variation. h. 10"-11". $30-40 each.

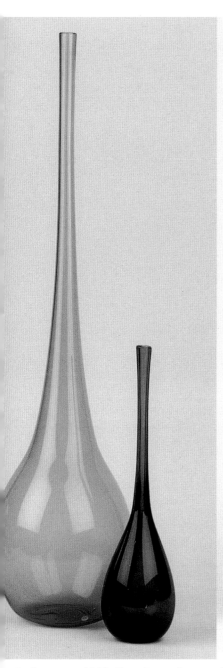

Anderson, c. 1949. Experimental vases with extra long slender necks, in Light Amethyst and Emerald,. h. 24". *Courtesy of Winlsow Anderson.*

#6427 bottle-vases. Myers 1964, design 27. Very cool extra tall bottle-vases with heavy bases, in Lemon and Tangerine. h. 25-1/2". $200-300 each.

#5616-B bottle. Husted 1956, design 16. Tangerine elongated bottle shown with #6427 bottle-vase in ruby crackle. h. 15". $30-40; $200-300.

#6427 bottle-vases in 1964 *House & Garden.* *Courtesy of Blenko.*

Blenko advertisement for #6427 with companion decanters #6425 (flame stopper) and #6426 (cylinder stopper). $150-175 each decanter.

#6937 tall bottle. Myers 1969, design 37. Olive Green cylindrical bottle-vase with long neck and flat collar; shown with long horn. h. 22-1/4". *Courtesy of Shirley Friedland.* $200-250.

#6937 in Blenko blue crackle. *Courtesy of Blenko.* $200-250.

#7223 tall vase. Nickerson 1972, design 23. Stretched bottle-vase in Blenko blue and irregular opening, shown with similar #64-B to show relative size. h. 25". $100-125.

Left: #6928 swirl vase. Myers 1969, design 28. Tangerine vase with optic swirl added to the similar earlier vase, with flared top and base. h. 20-1/4". *Courtesy of Mitchell Attenson.* $100-150.

Right: #6928 in Turquoise and Red $100-150 each.

Bottom left: Detail of optic.

#5516 giant bottle. One of Husted's "big-ass Blenko" designs (also available with button stopper); shown with "normal" sized Blenko bottle for comparison. h. 31". $300-400.

#5717 tall vase. Husted 1957, design 17. Jade green cylindrical pipe vase with two sections. h. 24". *Courtesy of the Huntington.* $200-250.

#5716 Bamboo vase. Husted 1957, design 16. Four-section cylindrical vase in Gold, inspired by the natural plant form—hence the name Bamboo vase; (shown with Bischoff #720.) h. 19-1/2". $150-200.

Different version of Blenko bamboo vase in Tangerine, shown with #5716 Bamboo vase and Nickerson's #7727, also with bamboo-like ring. h. 15". $100-150.

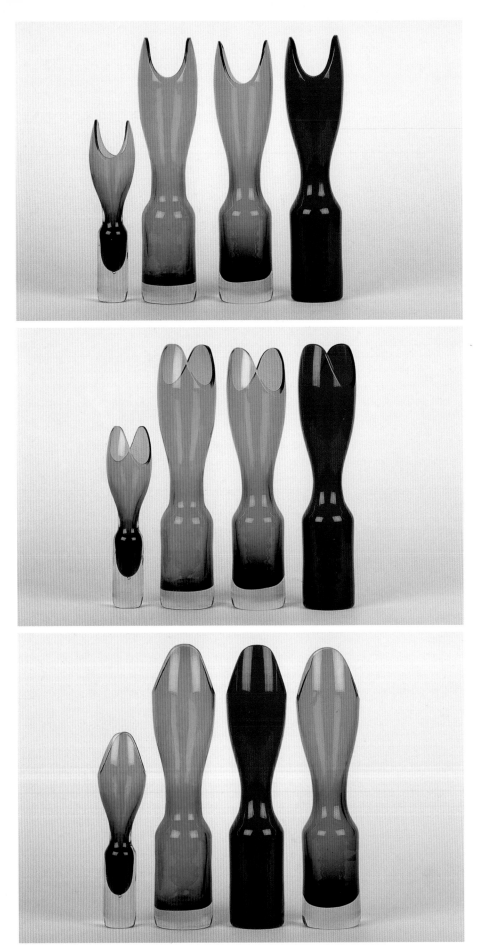

Husted classic #5915-S and #915-L bud vase/candleholders, with cut rim, in Turquoise, Ruby, and Nile. h. 9-1/2 and 12-1/2" $125-150; $250-350 each

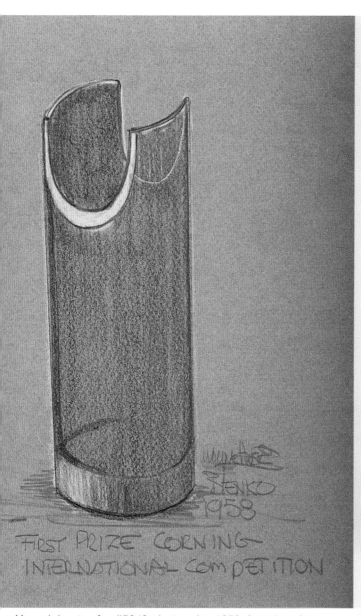

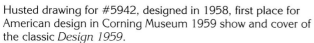

Husted drawing for #5942, designed in 1958, first place for American design in Corning Museum 1959 show and cover of the classic *Design 1959*.

#5942 cylindrical vase. Husted 1959, design 42. Award-winning vase with heavy crystal base and cut and ground top, in Jonquil and Lilac. h. 16". *Courtesy of the Huntington.* $300-400 each.

Top left: #6712 vase. Myers 1967, design 12. Later version of early experimental piece, in hourglass or barbell form with applied spiral in center. h. 11-1/4". $100-150.

Top right: #474 vase. Anderson 1947, design 4. Crystal vase with applied Ruby spiral; shown with highball in same style. *Courtesy of the Huntington.* $150-250.

Bottom: Anderson c. 1950. #915 pitcher and two different vases, all in crystal with applied spirals. *Courtesy of Winslow Anderson.* $200-250 each.

Opposite page:
Top: Anderson highball with later examples of applied spirals.

Bottom left: #6833-LT & #6833-CH vases. Myers 1968, design 33. Bottle-vases with ruffle top and applied threading in Lemon with Tangerine and Crystal with Honey. h. 10-1/4". $65-85.

Bottom right: Detail of threading.

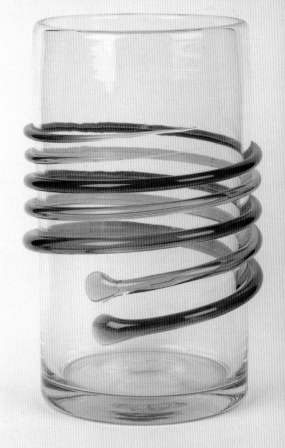

Top left: Bottle-vase with large applied spiral. *Courtesy of Blenko*. $75-95.

Top center: #6817-OT & #6817-TO vases. Myers 1968, design 17. Crackle finish bottle-vases in Olive Green with Turquoise spiral and Turquoise with Olive green spiral. h. 10". $80-100 each.

Top right: #6710A Tangerine and Honey applied spiral on crystal vase, shown on the cover of the 1967 Blenko Catalog. h. 9-1/2" $200-300

Left: #6815-OT vase. Myers 1968, design 15. Olive with Turquoise spiral, shown with similar design 6817 in crackle. h. 10". $80-100.

Myers experimental cylinder vase, 1965.

#659-L vase. Myers 1965, design 9. Honey cylindrical vase with weighted base and folded lip. h. 16". $80-100.

#15-TO & #14-TO Rialto vases. Husted 1960. Opalescent white vases with applied Tangerine bands at the opening, an unusual and rarely-seen Blenko design. h. 9-1/2" & 8-3/4". *Courtesy of Blenko.* $350-450; $300-350.

#12-TO Rialto vases. Husted 1960. Opalescent white vases with applied Tangerine bands around the middle. h. 8-1/2". *Courtesy of Blenko.* $350-450 each.

Anderson vase in red and crystal, designed in 1947, but produced only in plain colors. *Courtesy of Winslow Anderson.*

#905 pitcher-vase. Anderson, c. 1950. Ruby vase with pinched pouring spout. h. 10-3/4". *Courtesy of Winslow Anderson.* $75-95.

#6731 flattened Tangerine vase with textured surface. h. 10-1/4" $150-175

#828 Balloons. Shepherd 1982, design 8. Crystal with Lemon and Honey with Tangerine swirled Balloons. h. 11". *Courtesy of Blenko.* $125-175 each.

Top: #439-SL vase. 1943, design 39. Smaller of a series of vases with applied leaves and rosettes, in Crystal crackle with four Turquoise rosettes. h. 8". $70-90.

Bottom: #427-S beaker vase. 1942, design 7. Wild Rose beaker vase in blue with applied roses, and one of the scarcer designs with applied decoration. h. 8-1/2". $125-175.

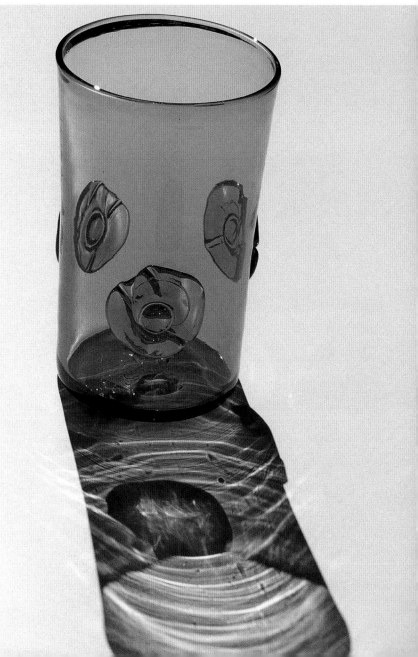

#473 Ear or Rope vase. 1947, design 3. Crystal crackle vase with applied Turquoise "ears" or ropes. h. 7-1/2". *Courtesy of the Huntington.* $75-100.

#473 Ear vase. Crystal with applied green ears. h. 7-1/2". $75-100.

Variation of #473 Ear vase in Chartreuse. h. 7". $75-100.

#366-ML & #473 vases. 1936, design 6. Crystal crackle medium-sized vase with applied amber leaves, a relatively common yet very collectible early design made in numerous color combinations from 1936-1965 (with dark green on crystal reintroduced in the '90s); with #473 Crystal crackle with Sea Green wings. *Courtesy of Blenko.* $75-100.

Variant of #473 with flared top, in Turquoise with Crystal wings. *Courtesy of Blenko.* $100-125.

Left: #366-SL vase. Small leaf vase in Tangerine with same color applied leaves. h. 7-1/2". *Courtesy of the Huntington.* $80-100.

Right: #366-LL vase. Large leaf vase in Crystal crackle with Sea Green leaves, shown with small size for comparison. h. 13". $100-150.

Small leaf vases in Turquoise crackle with same color leaves, and Crystal crackle with green leaves. h. 7-1/2". $60-90 ea.

Top: #986 vase. Anderson c. 1952. Large emerald green vase, in the shape of a water goblet, with applied blobs. h. 11". *Courtesy of Blenko.* $150-250.

Bottom: #479 footed vase. 1947, design 9. Crystal crackle vase (*right*) with applied green foot and rosettes, (shown with Crystal crackle vase with Crystal blobs, cocktail with Amethyst rosettes, and highball with Chartreuse spiral). h. 9-1/2". *Courtesy of Blenko.* $100-125.

Top: #404-S in Blenko blue and Chartreuse. $35-45 each.

Bottom left: #404-S & #404-M vases. Jonquil crackle and Amethyst crackle. h. 9" & 11-1/2". $35-45; $70-90.

Bottom right: #404-S & #404-L vases. 1940, design 4. Long-lasting design (1940-1965) of flared vase with pinched top, in Rosé crackle (1963-64) and Charcoal, both unusual colors. h. 9" & 15". *Courtesy of Blenko.* $60-80; $125-150 as shown.

1940-1965

#6949, #6115-L, & #607 rectangular vases. Myers 1969, design 49; Husted 1961, design 15; Husted 1960, design 7. Tangerine textured vase with four deep circular indentations; Sea Green heavy vase with ground top edge and molded stylized floral motif on sides; Tangerine vase with undulating sides and scalloped top. h. 12-1/2", 14-1/2", & 10". $100-150; $100-150; $60-80.

#6536 & #6520 vases. Myers 1965, designs 36 & 20. Tangerine cylindrical vase with dented sides and flat collar *(courtesy of Darlene Jupp)*; and Soldier vase with molded toy soldier on one of the four sides and flat collar. h. 23-1/2" & 18". $150-250 each.

#6420 jar-vase. Myers 1964, design 20. Large Tangerine jar-shaped vase with vertical ridged texture. h. 12". $100-150.

#6223 & #6222 textured vases. Husted 1962, designs 23 & 22. Tangerine vase with ridged texture and four sides with round opening, and Sea Green ridged vase (with #6420 jar). h. 12-1/2" & 9". $60-80; $50-70.

#384 water jar-vase. Probably the most common
Blenko item, still in the line after over 60 years.
h. 7-1/2". $25-35 each.

#6041 & #6046 bubble-wrap vases. Husted 1960, designs 41 & 46. Very cool bubbled surface vases in Tangerine and Jonquil, with sandblasted signature. h. 10-1/2" & 7-1/2". $75-100; $50-75 (+signature).

Top: #6010 vase. Husted 1960, design 10. Rarely seen design of Blenko blue cylindrical vase with pulled and folded petal-like top; with sandblasted signature. h. 10-3/4". $100-125 (+signature).

Bottom: #6042-B Vineyard vase. Husted 1960, design 42. Amethyst rose bowl form with overall bubble texture. h. 5-1/4". *Courtesy of Blenko.* $40-50.

Top: #6039 Lilac bubble wrap vase. h. 13-1/2" $150-200

Bottom: #3623 Cobweb vase. 1936, design 23. Rare design of cylindrical vase with overall "cobweb" pattern in Amethyst (made only 1936-37). h. 8". *Courtesy of the Huntington.* $200-250.

*In the pattern called* —

**Vineyard**

Available in Tangerine, Jonquil, Persian, Seagreen, Turquoise, Lilac, and Crystal. Prices are retail. Slightly higher west of the Rockies.

| 6045 | 6047-P | 6051 | 6042-B |
|------|--------|------|--------|
| 8½" Bowl | 6¼" Pitcher | 8" Water | 5¼" Bowl |
| $8.50 | $4.00 | Bottle | $4.00 |
| | | $3.00 | |

| 6049 | 6047-B | 6050 | 6048 | 6042-P |
|------|--------|------|------|--------|
| 11¾" Goblet | 3¾" Bowl | 5¾" Tumbler | 8¾" Goblet | 6¼" Pitcher |
| $9.00 | $2.50 | $2.00 | $6.50 | $5.00 |

BLENKO GLASS CO., INC.
Milton, West Virginia

Top left: Advertisement for Vineyard line.

Top right: #597 vase. Husted 1959, design 7. Very cool rounded vase with applied globs, in Lilac, with sandblasted signature. h. 5". *Courtesy of the Huntington.* $150-250.

Bottom left: #5940 vase. Husted 1959, design 40. Variation of rounded vase with flatter blobs, in Persian, with sandblasted signature. $125-150.

Bottom right: #622M vase. Husted 1962, design 2. Crystal barrel vase with applied Wheat "cookies." h. 7-3/8". $75-100.

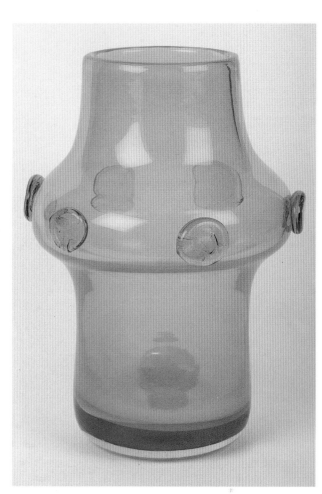

Top: #5935 vase in Jonquil with applied blobs around center. h. 9-1/2"
$125-175.

Bottom: $5935 and #597 Turquoise vases with blobs. h. 9-1/2 and 5".
*Photo courtesy of Gordon Harrell.*
$125-175, $150-250.

Top: #3615-L, #3615-S, & #3615X globe vases. 1936, design 15. Large Turquoise, small Ruby, and miniature Amethyst globe vases, easy to distinguish from the countless copies because of the colors and pontil mark. h. 8-1/2", 5", & 3". $100-125; $35-45; $15-20.

Bottom left: #3615-M globe vase. Sea Green medium globe vase, shown with horn vase. 6-1/2". $50-60.

Bottom right: Anderson globe vases, designed in 1947, in green seed glass and red swirl on crystal (not produced). *Courtesy of Winslow Anderson.*

Top: #961-S & #961-L flat-sided vases. Anderson c. 1950, design 1. Flat-sided vases with polished rims in Ruby, Emerald green, and light green, either seed glass or with slightly textured polished surface. h. 6" & 9". *Courtesy of Winslow Anderson.* $75-100; $150-200 each.

Bottom left: Olive Green and Chartreuse round vases by Anderson, c. 1950. *Courtesy of Blenko.* $50-60; $70-90.

Bottom right: Anderson's wide flat-sided vase in green. *Courtesy of Winslow Anderson.* $150-250.

#535 pouch vases in both 11" and 14" sizes. $150-175 and $200-300

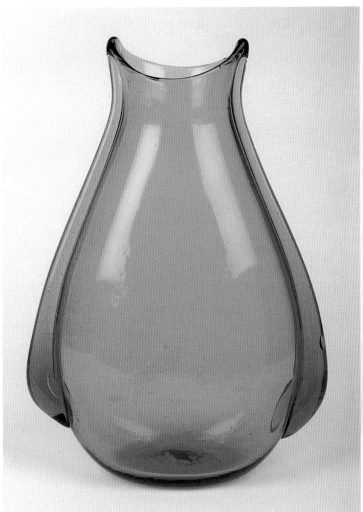

#534 pouch-shaped vase. Anderson c. 1950, design 4. Very cool Sea Green pouch-shaped vase with sheared rim and applied "fins." h. 11". $150-175.

#535 pouch-shaped vase. Anderson c. 1950, design 5. Emerald green vase with slightly wider body but same sheared rim and applied fins. h. 11". *Courtesy of the Huntington.* $150-175.

Amethyst flattened vase and Chartreuse long-necked flattened vase, designed by Anderson c. 1950, but not shown in Blenko catalogs. *Courtesy of Winslow Anderson.* $150-250; $100-125.

#6735 flattened vases. Myers 1967, design 35. Crystal and Olive Green vases with textured surface and thin neck of varying heights cut at an angle. h. 16-1/2" & 14-1/2". $75-125 each.

Top: #6517 vase. Myers 1965, design 17. Wide Tangerine vase with flared mouth; shown with candle-vase for relative size. h. 11". $50-60.

Bottom: #6735 flat vase in Plum, with narrow neck and diagonally cut rim.
$100-125

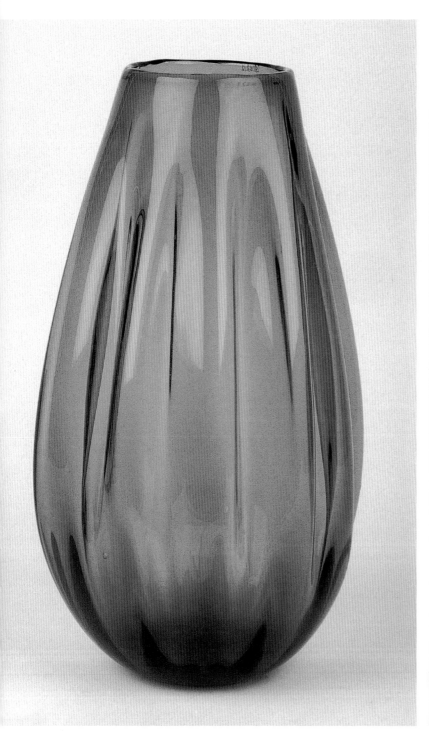

#942 free-form vase. Amber production piece. h. 13".
*Courtesy of Winslow Anderson.* $125-150.

#6421 Peacock molded vase with flat rim. h. 16"
$175-225

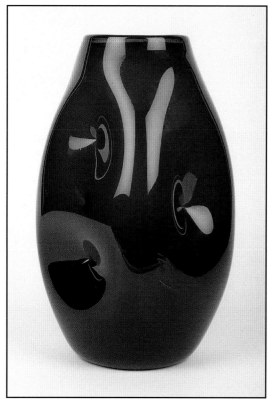

Top left: #949-S & #921-M indented vases. Anderson c. 1950. Turquoise and Sea Green indented vases. h. 6" & 10". $35-45; $70-90.

Top right: #921-L indented vase. Anderson c. 1950. Deep Emerald green heavy indented vase; a variation of this vase was used for Anderson's LP-11 lamp. h. 14". $125-175.

Bottom: #949-L aquarium vase. Anderson c. 1950. #949-L large and heavy Amethyst indented aquarium vase (shown with #949-S for relative size). h. & d. 13-1/2". $200-250.

#949-M, #921-L, & #910-4 indented vases. Emerald green and Blue medium round indented vases, with Turquoise tall vase (with polished rim), and more regular four-dent vase with lip. h. 7", 12", & 5-1/4". *Courtesy of Winslow Anderson.* $50-60; $175-225; $40-50.

#533 indented bud vase. Anderson 1953, design 3. One of Anderson's last Blenko designs, Sea Green indented bud vase, shown with four-dent vase and #487 crimped top vase. 7". $25-35.

#533 in Sea Green crackle. h. 7". $25-35.

#928 bud vases. Anderson c. 1950. Jonquil and Amethyst bud vases, shown with unusual Turquoise and green #533 indented bud vase. h. 5-1/2". *Courtesy of Winslow Anderson.* $25-35.

Detail of two-color combination.

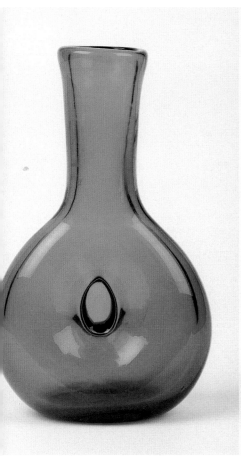

#441-L squat bottle vase. 1941, design 1. Deep Sea Green vase with pinched center. h. 7". $40-50.

Side view.

#7141 bottle vase. Myers 1971, design 41. Larger reintroduction of '40s design in Charcoal. *Courtesy of the Huntington.* $40-50.

#538 crimped bowl. Anderson 1953, design 8. Rose
bowl with crimped rim in Tangerine and an unusual
shade of greenish amber. h. 4". $30-40 each.

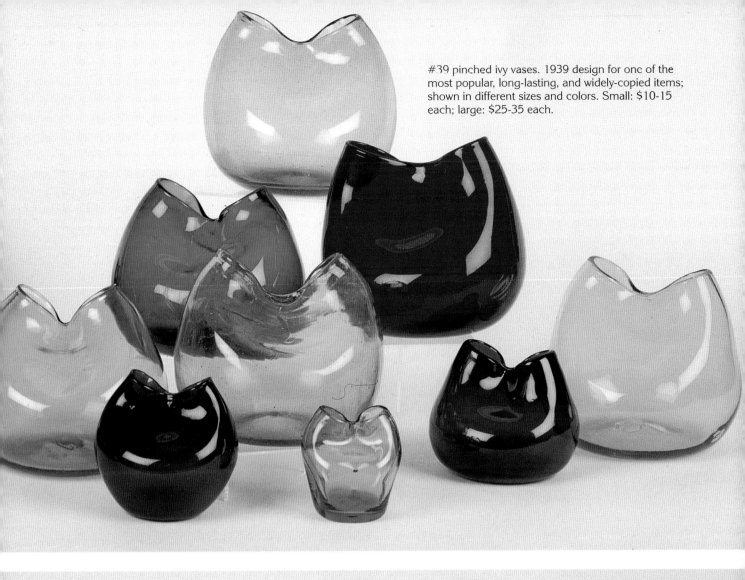

#39 pinched ivy vases. 1939 design for one of the most popular, long-lasting, and widely-copied items; shown in different sizes and colors. Small: $10-15 each; large: $25-35 each.

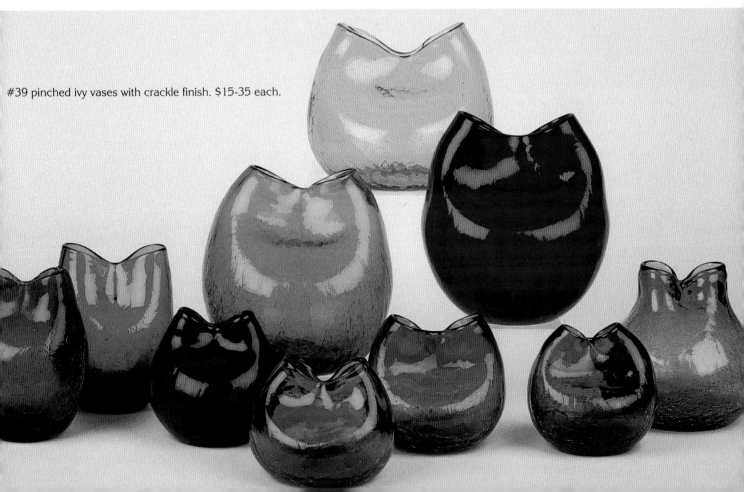

#39 pinched ivy vases with crackle finish. $15-35 each.

Bowl with only three crimps, shown with vase and ashtray all in unusual translucent burgundy. *Courtesy of Blenko.*

#415-S pinched vase. 1941, design 5. Taller version of ivy vase with pinched top to make a double opening. h. 6-1/2". $25-35.

#4695 lily vase. Sky blue lily vase with ball between the foot and vase, which distinguishes it from those made by other companies. h. 9-1/2". *Courtesy of Blenko.* $35-45.

#390 crimped top vase. Sea Green vase with bulbous bottom and flaring top portion with crimping. h. 8". *Courtesy of Blenko.* $45-55.

#487 crimped top vase. Anderson 1948, design 7. Chartreuse footed vase with ruffled and crimped top, one of the most popular and enduring designs; with #390 vase in Amethyst. h. 8". $40-50.

#388 crimped top vase. 1938, design 8. Almost identical to the 487 vase, but slightly shorter, shown in an unusual two-tone of Crystal crackle with Turquoise foot and applied rim. h. 7-1/2". *Courtesy of Blenko.* $75-85.

#629-M compotes. Husted 1962, design 9. Tangerine, Jonquil, and Olive Green footed compotes. $40-50 each.

Center left: #428-S footed vases. 1942, design 8. Turquoise and Ruby bell-shaped footed vases h. 7". *Courtesy of Blenko.* $45-55 each.

Bottom left: #58-L bell vase in Sea Green seed glass, 1940s. h. 9". $60-70.

Right: #487 in Sea Green. $40-50.

Top: Group of Blenko #3516 series and other early miniatures, most in crackle. Unlike Pilgrim, Rainbow, and other companies that produced most of the miniatures on the market in the 1950s-70s, Blenko made fewer of them and earlier. $15-25 each.

Bottom left: Crackle miniatures. $15-25 each.

Bottom center: Crackle miniatures. $15-25 each.

Bottom right: CM-6 crackle miniatures. $15-20 each.

Crackle miniatures in Blenko colors (Bischoff made the identical model). $15-20 each.

CM-3 & CM-5 crackle miniature. $15-25 each.

CM-3 with #6422 to show both relative size and similarity of form of base.

#57-F miniature. Husted's 1957 design for miniature vase in same shape as his #563 mushroom decanter (shown with smaller stopper); each miniature in this series was made in only one color, this one in Tangerine. h. 5" (& 14"). $25-35; ($100-150).

# Chapter 6

# Handles

#6526 large jugs. Myers 1965, design 26. Honey crackle and Blenko blue large jugs with long neck. h. 15-1/4". $75-125 each.

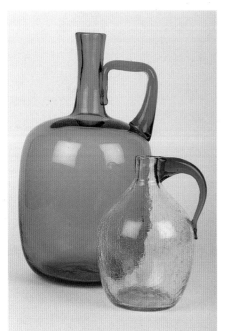

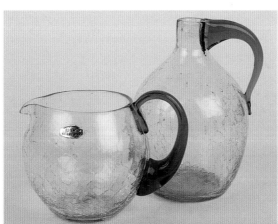

#3750-L pitcher. 1937, design 50. Pitcher in Crystal crackle with Turquoise handle, one of the most enduring designs (larger version is #361P, 7-1/2" tall); shown with #417 jug. $35-45.

#417 jug. 1941, design 7. Crystal crackle jug with Turquoise handle; shown with #6526 to show relative size. h. 8". $35-45.

#417 Chartreuse jug, reintroduced as #7117. h. 8". $35-45.

Chartreuse with narrow base, designed by Anderson c. 1948. *Courtesy of Winslow Anderson.* $50-60.

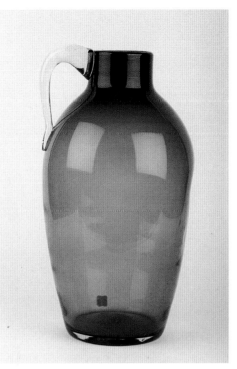

#443 large jug. 1944, design 3. Tall Charcoal jug with applied Crystal handle. h. 17-1/2". *Courtesy of Blenko.* $125-175.

Probably an early Blenko jug in Turquoise crackle with applied prunts, or raspberries. *Courtesy of the Huntington.* $60-80.

#5424 jug. Husted 1954, design 24. Sea Green jug with flattened handle. h. 11-3/4". $75-100.

#5424 crackle jug in unusual honey-amber color. $75-100.

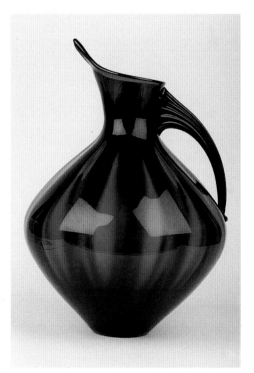

#963 optic pitcher. Anderson c. 1950. Large Emerald green pitcher with bulbous body and narrow base, a more elegant form than the #991 pitcher that became so popular. h. 14". *Courtesy of Winslow Anderson.* $150-200.

123

#584 and 585 sculpted pitchers in Gold and Mulberry. h. 7-3/4 and 9-1/4". *Photo courtesy of Gordon Harrell.*
$225-300, $300-400.

#991 in green with Crystal handle (*left*), no optic, an unusual version modified by Husted and shown in catalogs only around 1960; shown with optic versions. $80-100.

Top left: #418P dented pitcher. 1941, design 8. Ruby cylindrical pitcher with random dents; with #939P pitcher. h. 11". *Courtesy of the Huntington.* $60-80.

Bottom left: #939P in Tangerine crackle and Honey, showing variation in mouth opening. $70-90 each.

Top right: #939P pitcher. Anderson c. 1950. Popular pitcher with slanted opening that shows considerable variation in width, shown in Ruby. (The narrow is the more elegant design and desirable item.) h. 14-1/2". $70-90.

Bottom right: #939P pitcher in *House & Garden* August 1949 advertisement. *Courtesy of Blenko.*

#967 flat-sided pitcher. Anderson c. 1950. Elegantly proportioned flat-sided pitcher with slanted mouth in Sea Green, Ice Blue, and light Tangerine; the slant is achieved by trimming the top edge with shears while the glass is still hot. h. 12". *Courtesy of Winslow Anderson.* $125-175 each.

Top: #5828-L optic pitcher. Husted 1958, design 28. Jonquil optic pitcher with applied disc base, made only in 1958 and 1959; with sandblasted signature. h. 11". $100-125.

Bottom: #967 in Chartreuse. $125-175.

Top: Ruby miniature pitcher. *Courtesy of Blenko.* $15-25 each.

Center left: #3750-L pitchers. 1937, design 50. Tangerine pitchers in popular design. h. 5-1/2". *Courtesy of the Huntington.* $30-40 each.

Center right: #361P pitcher (larger version of #3750-L) in Crystal crackle with Ruby handle; shown with Ruby miniature to show relative size. h. 7". *Courtesy of Blenko.* $35-55.

#361P with mug in same colors.
*Courtesy of Blenko.*

#361P in Sea Green crackle. $35-45.

Poorly formed #361P in green with Crystal handle. $25-35.

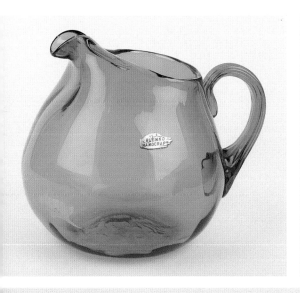

Top left: One of Husted's many pitcher designs from the 1950s, in Blenko Blue. *Courtesy of Blenko.* $55-65.

Top right: One of Husted's many pitcher designs from the 1950s, in Chartreuse; shown with tumblers. h. 7-1/4". *Courtesy of Blenko.* $35-45.

Bottom: Tangerine spittoon, not found in the catalog, but definitely Blenko. h. 5-1/2", d. 8-1/2". $50-70.

129

#5711 footed pitcher. Husted 1957, design 11. Tangerine cylindrical pitcher on hollow foot, one of the early footed series. h. 13-1/2". $125-150.

Rialto 6-TO pitcher. Husted 1960. Tall pitcher in opaque white with Ruby handle, made only in 1960. h. 14". *Courtesy of Blenko* $350-450.

#6714 indented pitcher. Myers 1967, design 14. Wheat crackle pitcher with random dents and pinched spout. h. 10". $35-45.

Early ewer or two-handled vase in Cobalt. h. 8". *Courtesy of Blenko.* $70-90.

Early cruet in Cobalt, shown with other Cobalt items. *Courtesy of Blenko.* $30-40.

#919-C footed cruet. Anderson c. 1950. Cruet with flame stopper in Sea Green. h. 9". *Courtesy of Blenko.* $60-70.

Top left: #948 bent neck decanter. Anderson c. 1950. Very cool classic Blenko design, recipient of the "Good Design Award" and widely copied (identified as Blenko by color, handle placement, and stopper); button stopper in Turquoise and smaller version in Sea Green. h. 13" & 9". *Courtesy of the Huntington.* $125-175; $70-90 small.

Bottom left: Anderson experimental sculptural pitcher, done by altering tall Sea Green vase. *Courtesy of Winslow Anderson.*

Top right: #948 in Amethyst with #497CT cocktail. *Courtesy of the Huntington.* $125-175.

Bottom right: Anderson Crystal cocktail mixer with brown handle and stirrer. *Courtesy of Winslow Anderson.* $70-90.

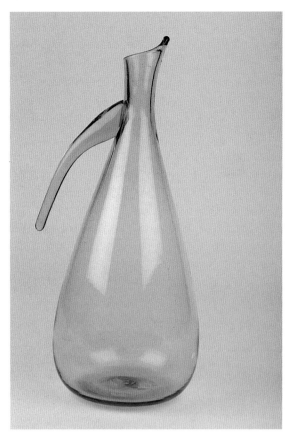

Top left: #5311 pitcher. Anderson 1953, design 11. Sea Green pitcher, or decanter when used with a cork. h. 12". *Courtesy of Winslow Anderson.* $100-150.

Top right: #968 chianti bottle decanter. Anderson c. 1950. Tall chianti wine style pitcher-decanter, shown with corks in Lemon and Blenko blue. h. 16-1/4". *Courtesy of Winslow Anderson.* $100-150 each.

Bottom left: #968 chianti bottle pitcher-decanter in Sea Green and deep leaf green. $100-150 each.

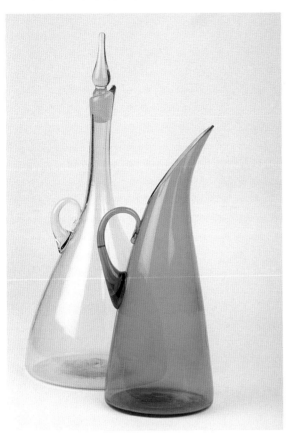

Top left: Anderson experimental decanter and pitcher. *Courtesy of Winslow Anderson.*

Top right: #976 tall pitcher. Anderson c. 1950. Tall tapering pitcher with long slated spout in Sea Green, shown with glasses. h. 19-1/2". *Courtesy of Blenko.* $100-125.

Bottom left: #976 pitcher in Ruby with extra long spout. *Courtesy of Blenko.* $100-125.

Bottom right: #976 pitchers in Lilac and Tangerine. $100-125 each.

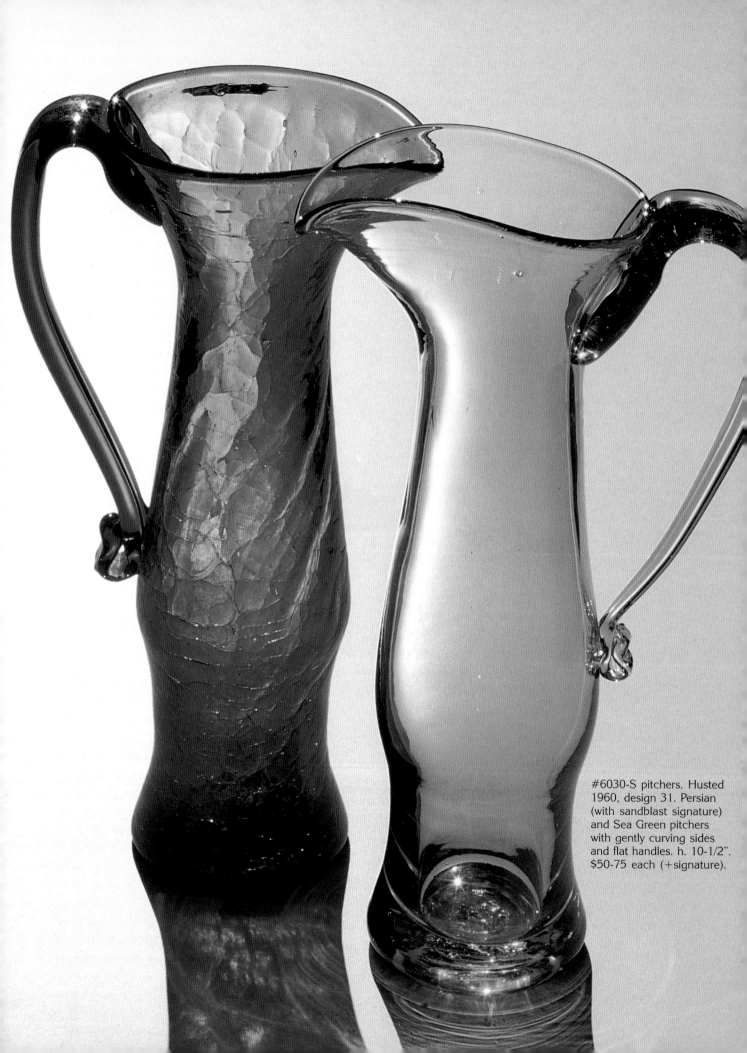

#6030-S pitchers. Husted
1960, design 31. Persian
(with sandblast signature)
and Sea Green pitchers
with gently curving sides
and flat handles. h. 10-1/2".
$50-75 each (+signature).

Husted 1959, design 26. #5926-S pitcher. Sea Green pitcher with flat handle, shown with #6030 flat-handled pitcher. h. 9". $50-60.

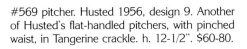

#5710 pitcher. Husted 1957, design 10. Earlier design with more pronounced curves than the #6030, in Blenko blue. h. 15". *Courtesy of Blenko*. $125-175.

#569 pitcher. Husted 1956, design 9. Another of Husted's flat-handled pitchers, with pinched waist, in Tangerine crackle. h. 12-1/2". $60-80.

Top left: #656-M pitcher (*center*). Myers 1965, design 11 (shown with #6511 & #7111). h. 11-1/2". $60-70.

Top right: #7111 pitchers. Myers 1971, design 11 (designed 1970). Blenko blue pitcher with smaller version, not in catalog. h. 12" & 10". $50-60 each.

Bottom left: #7033 pitchers. Myers 1970, design 33. Large Tangerine optic pitchers with bulbous bottom, stove-pipe neck, and oversized flat ribbon handle. h. 16-1/2". 125-175 each.

Bottom right: #7033 with #6511 pitcher to show relative size.

#6511 pitchers. Myers 1965, design 11. Tangerine and Blenko blue optic pitchers with wide cylindrical base and narrower neck. h. 9-1/2". $50-60 each.

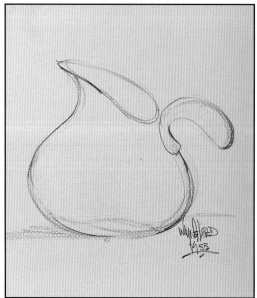

Top left: #5611 pitcher. Husted 1956, design 11. Odd pitcher with pinched waist and knobby lever handle, in leafy green. h. 9". $50-60.

Top right: #573 cocktail pitcher with stopper, in Tangerine. h. 11". *Photo courtesy of Gordon Harrell.* $250-350.

Left: Husted drawing for #555 pitcher—with same lever handle as 5611.

138

Top left: "Swish-it" cocktail mixers/pitchers in Chartreuse and Turquoise, designed by Anderson by adding whimsical handle to his #905 vase. *Courtesy of Winslow Anderson.* $125-150 each.

Bottom left: #6835-LT pitcher, Lemon with Tangerine applied rope. h. 17-1/2" $175-225
Photo courtesy of Gordon Harrell

Top right: Anderson pitcher in teapot form with long spout, in Ruby. *Courtesy of Winslow Anderson.*

Bottom center: #6814 pitcher. Myers 1968, design 14. Crystal pitcher (same form as #6815 vase) with applied Turquoise spiral and handle. h. 10". *Courtesy of Mitchell Attenson.* $80-100.

Bottom right: Detail.

# Chapter 7

# Drinkware

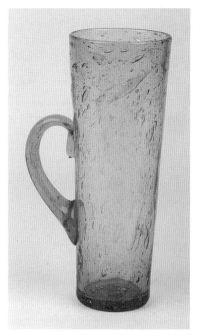 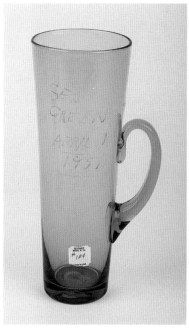 

Top left: #3627-H chimney hiball. 1936, design 27. Sea Green seed glass with handle. h. 9". *Courtesy of the Huntington.* $20-30.

Top center: Chimney hiball with handle, marked in crayon "sea green April 1, 1951" and with Blenko sticker. *Courtesy of Blenko.*

Top right: Turquoise example with poorly-made handle.

Center: Blenko blue crackle large mugs (24-oz. capacity), with foil sticker, but not pictured in catalog. h. 4-1/2". $20-25 each.

Bottom left: #515-G mugs. Anderson 1951, design 5. Crystal mugs with applied brown rings and handle. *Courtesy of Blenko.* $25-35 each .

Bottom right: #922 mug (*right*). Anderson c. 1950. Crystal mug with applied Turquoise spirals, with #515G mug with Sea Green rings. *Courtesy of Blenko.* $30-35.

Top left: #3749 hiballs. Crystal hiballs with applied green and Cobalt rings. These examples were made in 1999 but not for the line, and have later Blenko sticker. $20-25 each.

Bottom left: #448-R ringed old fashioned. 1944, design 8. Chartreuse seed glass with Ruby ring, a rare combination. $30-40 each.

Bubbles in seed glass seen on reflection.

Top left: #448-R ringed old fashioned. Crystal with different colored rings. $20-25 each.

Bottom left: #600-OF old fashioned. Anderson c. 1950. Crystal old fashioned glasses with Sea Green spirals. *Courtesy of Blenko.* $25-30 each.

Top right: Cover of 1967 catalog showing vases with two-tone spirals.

Bottom right: #600-HB hiballs. Anderson c. 1950. Crystal crackle with Ruby spiral and crystal with unusual two-tone Tangerine spiral, shown with ringed hiball. h. 6-3/4". *Courtesy of Blenko.* $25-35 each.

#600-HB hiballs. Anderson c. 1950. Crystal with Ruby spirals. h. 6-3/4". $25-35 each.

Top: #600-CT cocktails. Anderson c. 1950. Emerald green with Chartreuse spiral. *Courtesy of Blenko*. $25-30 each.

Bottom left: Detail.

Bottom center: #600-DOF double old fashioned. Anderson c. 1950. Chartreuse seed glass with emerald green spiral. *Courtesy of Blenko*. $25-35.

Bottom right: Hiball, old fashioned, and double hiball with applied decorations.

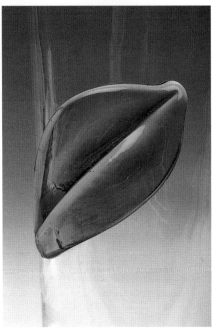

Top: #3627-L chimney hiballs. Crystal with applied leaf in six different colors. h. 9". $30-35 each.

Bottom left: Detail.

Bottom right: Chimney hiball in Chartreuse seed glass with Ruby leaf; Chartreuse cocktail with Ruby leaf. *Courtesy of the Huntington.* $35-40; $30-35.

#3627-L chimney hiballs in Chartreuse seed glass with green leaf. *Courtesy of Blenko.* $35-40 each.

Chartreuse seed glass cocktail with green leaf. *Courtesy of Blenko.* $30-35 each.

Double old fashioned, chimney hiball, and cocktail in Chartreuse seed glass with green leaf. *Courtesy of Blenko.* $30-40 each.

Chartreuse tumblers in cylindrical form. *Courtesy of Blenko.* $15-20 each.

#3627 chimney hiballs in Sea Green, Amethyst, Turquoise, and Chartreuse. *Courtesy of the Huntington.* $20-25 each.

Left: Chimney hiballs in Tangerine and Peacock. *Courtesy of Blenko.* $20-25 each.

Right: Chimney hiballs in Crystal crackle. $20-25 each.

Top left: #3753-HB with rosettes. Ice Blue 16-oz. hiball with pale Chartreuse cocktail with rosettes. $30-40 each.

Top right: Detail.

Bottom left: #3753 in pale Amethyst and pale brown. *Courtesy of Blenko*. $30-40 each.

Bottom center: Three different sizes with rosettes. *Courtesy of Blenko*. $30-40 each.

Bottom right: One-of-a-kind butterscotch #3753 rosette glass, made for the Blenko family. *Courtesy of Blenko*.

#445-HB & #445-0F rosette glasses. Chartreuse and Sea Green hiballs with applied rosettes, or raspberries; with sample cocktail with paper stickers "No. 7, July 8, 1948 good color chartreuse." *Courtesy of Blenko.* $30-40 each.

#445-CT cocktails. 1944, design 5. Turquoise cocktail glasses with applied rosettes. h. 2-1/2". $20-25 each.

#445-CT cocktails. 1944, design 5. Turquoise cocktail glasses. h. 2-1/2". $12-18 each.

#445-OF old fashioned. Sea Green old fashioned tumbler with cocktail. *Courtesy of Blenko.* $15-20.

#385 hiball. 1938, design 5. Brown and green 14-oz. hiballs. *Courtesy of the Huntington.* $20-25 each.

Variety of drinking glasses. *Courtesy of Blenko.* $15-30 each.

#361 beverage set. 1936, design 1. Sky Blue seed glass pitcher and six 12-oz. tumblers. h. 7-1/2" & 4". $175-225 set.

Reflection of seed glass.

150

Early Sea Green seed glass cocktail and juice tumblers. *Courtesy of Blenko.* $20-25 each.

Variety of Ruby drinkware. *Courtesy of Blenko.* $20-25 each.

#950-HB hiball & #950-CT cocktail. Anderson 1951. Crystal glasses with attached colored ashtray. h. 6-5/8" & 3-5/8". *Courtesy of Blenko.* $30-40 each.

#950-HB hiball & #950-CT cocktail. Anderson 1951. Crystal glasses with attached colored ashtray. h. 6-5/8" & 3-5/8". *Courtesy of Blenko.* $30-40 each.

#418-L tumblers. Blenko blue crackle indented tumblers. h. 6". $15-25 each.

#418-S tumblers. Olive Green crackle indented tumblers. h. 6". $15-20 each.

#418-L emerald green crackle indented tumblers. h. 4-1/2". $10-20 each.

Top: #418-L & #418-S tumblers. Tangerine, Jonquil, and Ruby indented tumblers. *Courtesy of Blenko.* $15-25 each.

Bottom left: #418-L tumblers. Sky Blue and emerald green indented tumblers. h. 6". $15-25 each.

Bottom right: #418-DOF double old fashioned. 1941, design 8. Tangerine crackle indented double old fashioned, discontinued in 1965. h. 4". $20-25.

Group of indented tumblers. *Courtesy of Blenko.* $15-25 each.

Variety of early colored stemware 1930s-1950. *Courtesy of Blenko*.

Variety of early wine goblets from the 1930s and #414 giant 8-1/2" water goblet (*center*) in Ruby. *Courtesy of Blenko*. $20-35 each; $45-55 giant.

Early wine glasses from the 1930s in emerald green. *Courtesy of Blenko*. $25-35 each.

Early wine glasses in Sky Blue. *Courtesy of Blenko*. $25-35 each.

#926 stems. Anderson c. 1950. Ruby bowl and Crystal stem and foot, with #700-S (*top*). *Courtesy of Blenko.* $25-40 each.

#800-S sherbets. Anderson c. 1950. Ruby bowl and foot and Crystal airtwist stem. *Courtesy of Blenko.* $30-50 each.

#800-S sherbets. Anderson c. 1950. Jonquil bowl and foot and Crystal airtwist stem. *Courtesy of Blenko.* $30-50 each.

Top left: #800 stems. Anderson c. 1950. Sherbet, wine, and goblet with emerald green bowl foot and Crystal airtwist stem. *Courtesy of Blenko.* $30-50 each.

Top right: Group of airtwist stemware with emerald green giant goblet. *Courtesy of Blenko.* $30-40 each; $75-120.

Bottom: #489 giant goblets. Anderson 1948, design 9. Persian (1959 with sandblast signature) bowl with Crystal airtwist stem and foot, with pale Lilac and Crystal giant goblets. h. 13". $75-125 each (+signature).

Left: #581 Sea Green large goblet. h. 12-1/4" $200-275 Photo courtesy of Gordon Harrell

Right: #5923 Aqua goblets. h. 11-1/4" $150-250 each Photo courtesy of Gordon Harrell

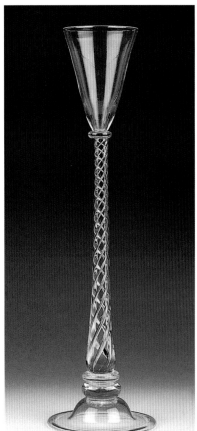

Left: Crystal wedding goblet with tall airtwist stem, designed by Anderson c. 1948 and in very limited production. *Courtesy of Winslow Anderson.* $150-200.

Right: #956 chalice. Anderson c. 1952. Emerald green chalice in hour-glass shape with crystal ball in the middle. h. 15-1/2". *Courtesy of Winslow Anderson.* $150-200 each.

# Chapter 8

# Tableware

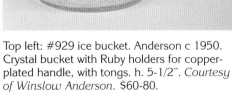

Top left: #929 ice bucket. Anderson c 1950. Crystal bucket with Ruby holders for copper-plated handle, with tongs. h. 5-1/2". *Courtesy of Winslow Anderson.* $60-80.

Bottom left: #996 & #995 utility jars. Anderson 1952. Winner of Museum of Modern Art "Good Design Award", in Crystal crackle with Chartreuse glass lid. h. 10-1/4" & 11-3/4". *Courtesy of Winslow Anderson.* $100-150 each.

Top right: Crystal cocktail mixer with Tangerine stirrer, designed by Anderson c. 1950. *Courtesy of Winslow Anderson.* $40-60.

Bottom right: Experimental decanter in Sky Blue seed glass, with cocktail. *Courtesy of the Huntington.*

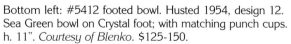

Bottom left: #5412 footed bowl. Husted 1954, design 12. Sea Green bowl on Crystal foot; with matching punch cups. h. 11". *Courtesy of Blenko.* $125-150.

Top: #925-PB punch bowl, #925-L ladle & #925-C cups. Anderson c. 1950. Ruby punch bowl with matching rim; ladle with Crystal handle and Ruby bowl; Crystal cups with applied Ruby handles. d. 10"; ladle l. 14". *Courtesy of Blenko.* $100-150; $70-90; $10-15 each.

Bottom right: #7043-L footed bowl. Myers 1970, design 43. Ruby rose bowl on Crystal conical base, made only 1970-71. h. 14". *Courtesy of Blenko.* $150-200.

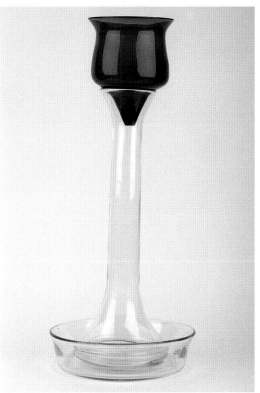

Top left: Shepherd design for centerpiece with bowl using the #789 vase in Crystal, in a Crystal bowl, with Cobalt top. h. 28". *Courtesy of Blenko*. $150-200.

Top right: #974 hollow stem compote. Anderson 1952. Pale blue bowl on hourglass shape base. h. 13-1/4". *Courtesy of Winslow Anderson*. $125-150.

Bottom: #6830-OT. Myers 1968, design 30. Olive Green epergne with applied Turquoise threading on ruffled edges of vase and bowl. h. 14", d. 15-1/2". *Courtesy of Blenko*. $150-250.

#6840 centerpiece bowl. Myers 1968, design 40. Tangerine footed bowl with scalloped rim. d. 15-1/2". $70-90.

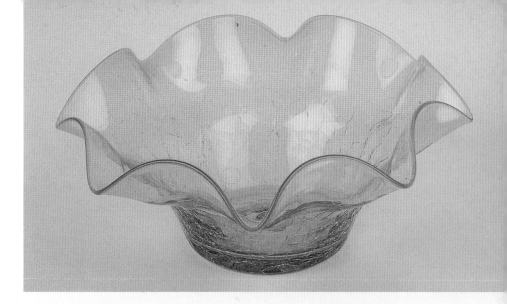

#3744-X scalloped bowl. Jonquil crackle bowl with scalloped rim. d. 7". $25-30.

#955-L asymmetrical bowl in Charcoal. $125-150

#5429 asymmetrical bowl. Husted 1954, design 29. Amethyst freeform bowl with graceful lines. l. 11". *Courtesy of Blenko.* $60-70.

#955-L asymmetrical bowl. Anderson 1952. Ruby freeform bowl with flowing lines coming to points. l. 17-1/2". $125-150.

Early green seed glass centerpiece bowl. *Courtesy of Blenko.* $70-90.

#445 bowl. Ruby bowl with applied raspberries. d. 8". *Courtesy of Blenko.* $60-70.

#445 bowl with applied raspberries in Sky Blue bubbled seed glass. d. 12". $80-100.

#932 serving bowl. Anderson c. 1950. Chartreuse crackle footed serving bowl. d. 8-1/2". *Courtesy of Winslow Anderson.* $50-60.

Small Sky Blue bowl with applied raspberries; shown with miniature bud vase and drinkware. *Courtesy of Blenko* $30-40.

#919-S sherbet. Anderson 1950. Crystal bowl with Ruby swirls and foot. h. 2-3/4". *Courtesy of Blenko.* $50-60.

Bird's-eye view.

Crystal bowl with Turquoise top; shown with Crystal vase with applied Turquoise band, probably 1970s. *Courtesy of Blenko.* $60-80 each.

Crystal crackle bowl with applied rim and three pinched sections, probably 1970s. d. 10". *Courtesy of Mitchell Attenson.* $50-70.

#901-L bowls. Anderson 1950. Ruby and Turquoise centerpiece bowls, winner of "Good Design Award." d. 13-1/2". *Courtesy of Winslow Anderson.* $125-175 each.

#5418 molded double tray. Husted 1954, design 18. Crystal tray with two sections in thick heavy textured glass; with experimental bowl. *Courtesy of Blenko.* $30-40.

#6023 bowl. Husted 1960, design 23. Heavy freeform Sea Green bowl, dumped out of a mold; with sandblasted signature. d. 7". $20-30 (+signature).

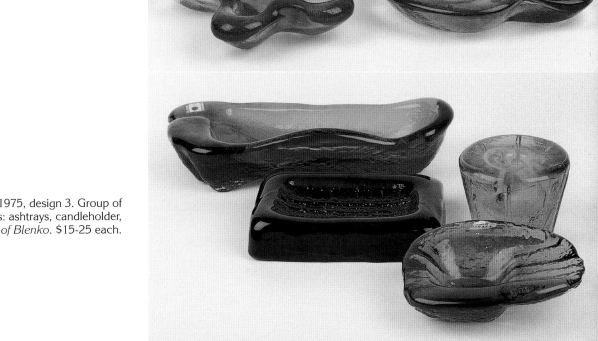

#966 freeform ashtrays. Anderson 1952. Cobalt and Jonquil heavy freeform ashtrays, dumped out of a mold. Average l. 8". $20-25 each.

#753 foot. Nickerson 1975, design 3. Group of heavy molded glass items: ashtrays, candleholder, and soap dish. *Courtesy of Blenko.* $15-25 each.

#951 asymmetrical ashtray. Anderson c. 1951. Heavy asymmetrical ashtray; with similar bowls. l. 6-1/2". *Courtesy of Blenko.* $15-30 each.

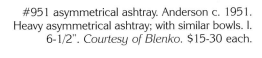

#5910 bowl. Husted 1959, design 10. Blenko blue bowl, made by slicing a blown piece in two and polishing the edges. l. 8-1/2". *Courtesy of Blenko.* $100-150.

Top: Turquoise #5910 and Jonquil #599 cut bowls. 8-1/4 and 17-1/2" $100-150, $175-225
*Photo courtesy of Gordon Harrell*

Bottom: Ruby #5924 ashtray/bowl with sheared ends, and #5927-L reversible bowl and candleholder. w. 9"
and h. 7" $175-250, $200-275
*Photo courtesy of Gordon Harrell*

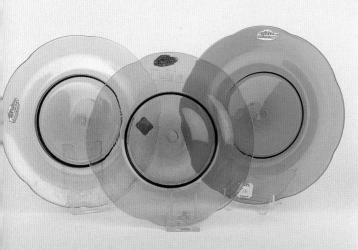

Top left: #5423 crimped bowl. Husted 1954, design 23. Shallow Ruby bowl with multi-crimped rim. d. 9-1/4". *Courtesy of Blenko.* $30-40.

Top right: #6143-S bowl. Husted 1961, design 43. Heavy molded floriform bowl, still being produced today in small and large sizes. $10-15.

Center: #19 plates. Anderson c. 1950. Sea Green, Amethyst, and Turquoise plates with slightly scalloped rims. d. 8". *Courtesy of Blenko.* $25-35 each.

Bottom left: #19 plate in Ruby. d. 10". *Courtesy of Blenko.* $40-50.

Bottom right: #7331 platter. Nickerson 1973, design 31. Large serving platter in green with yellow center and applied green rim. d. 18". *Courtesy of Blenko.* $100-150.

# Chapter 9

# Lighting

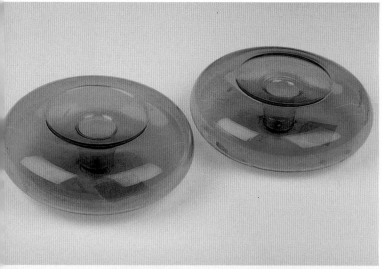

#902 candle holders. Anderson 1950. Round low Turquoise candle holders. d. 5-1/4". *Courtesy of Winslow Anderson.* $50-70 pair.

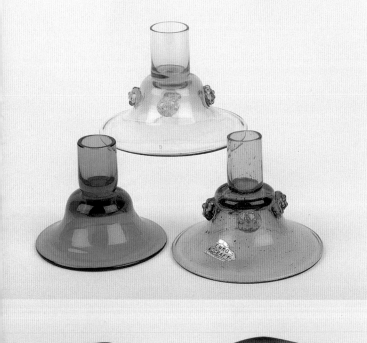

#445-CS candle holders. Turquoise plain and Sea Green and Chartreuse with rosettes. *Courtesy of Blenko.* $20-25; $30-35 each.

Early airtwist candle holders with Ruby top and Crystal base. *Courtesy of Blenko.* $70-90 pair.

Left: Experimental candle holder by Anderson in Ruby with rings and rosettes. *Courtesy of Winslow Anderson.*

Right: Crystal candle holder with applied facial features. *Courtesy of Blenko.* $25-30.

Bottom: Rialto #8-TO candle holder. Husted 1960. Opalescent white candle holder with Ruby trim; with Rialto #9-TO bowl. h. 7". *Courtesy of Blenko.* $350-450; $250-350.

Top: #476 console set. 1947, design 6. #476-CS candle sticks and #476-B center-piece bowl, in Crystal with applied Sea Green decoration. h. 7"; bowl d. 11-1/2". *Courtesy of Blenko.* $200-250 set.

Bottom left: #476-CS candlesticks in Crystal with Sky Blue and Ruby decoration. h. 7". *Courtesy of the Huntington.* $50-70 each.

Bottom right: #444-CS candlestick. 1944, design 4. Turquoise candlestick with twist stem and disc foot. h. 7". *Courtesy of Blenko.* $30-40.

Anderson's green candlesticks of tall vase with applied fins and separate candle insert; not pictured in catalogs. *Courtesy of Winslow Anderson.* $250-350 pair.

Detail of top.

Above: Anderson signature on twist candlestick.

Left: Anderson experimental candlestick of single twist of emerald green glass. *Courtesy of Winslow Anderson.*

Top: #6424 candle-vase. Myers 1964, design 24. One of Myers' first and most enduring design of a small bottle-vase that doubles as a candle holder, in Tangerine, green, and Chartreuse. h. 5". $25-35 each.

Bottom: 6424 in Tangerine, Olive Green, and Blenko Blue crackle. $25-35 each.

Top left: Catalog page with Anderson's LP-10 and LP-8 lamps. $125-175 each.

Bottom left: Catalog page with Anderson's LP-11 and LP-7 lamps. $125-175 each.

Right: LP-11 lamp in Charcoal with original finial and wood base. h. 27". $150-175.

Top right: Vintage photo of lamp display with LP-11 on top shelf. *Courtesy of Blenko.*

Top left: Catalog page with Anderson's LP-13 and LP-9 lamps. $150-175 each.

Bottom: LP-13 in emerald green. $300-350 pair (with finials).

Left: Vintage photo of McCreery's Blenko Glass Collection with lamps. *Courtesy of Blenko.*

Bottom left: Anderson Blenko blue crackle lamp base as a vase. *Courtesy of Winslow Anderson.*

Bottom right: Chartreuse lamp-in-a-bowl with original finial. $150-175.

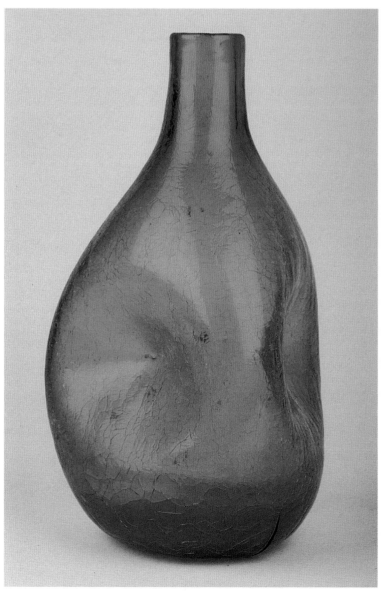

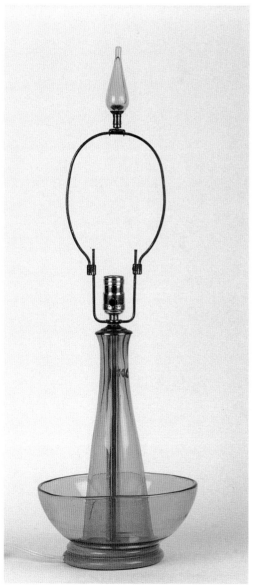

Catalog page with Anderson's LP-12 and LP-4 lamps. $100-125 each.

Catalog page with Anderson's LP-6 and LP-25 lamps. $100-125 each.

Catalog page with Anderson's LP-20 lamp. $125-175.

Catalog page with Anderson's LP-16 and LP-18 lamps. $125-175 each.

Catalog page with Anderson's LP-26, LP-43, and LP-24 lamps. $125-150 each.

LP-16
30 inches
over-all height

LP-18
34 inches
over-all height

LP-26
30 inches
over-all height

LP-19
43 inches
over-all height

LP-24
35 inches
over-all height

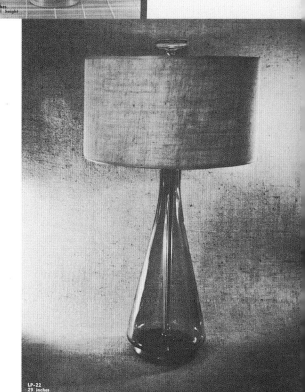

Catalog page with Anderson's LP-22 lamp. $125-150.

LP-22
29 inches
over-all height

# Chapter 10

# Figural & Others

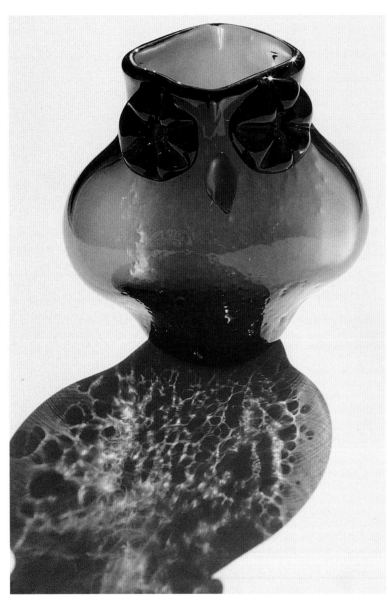

#5830-S owl vase. Husted 1958, design 30. Mulberry vase in the form of an owl, with applied rosette eyes, sandblast signature. h. 7". $350-500 (+signature).

#559 cat vase. Other character in Husted's "owl and the pussycat" duo, Charcoal cat with applied Crystal ears and handle. h. 13". *Courtesy of Blenko.* $400-500.

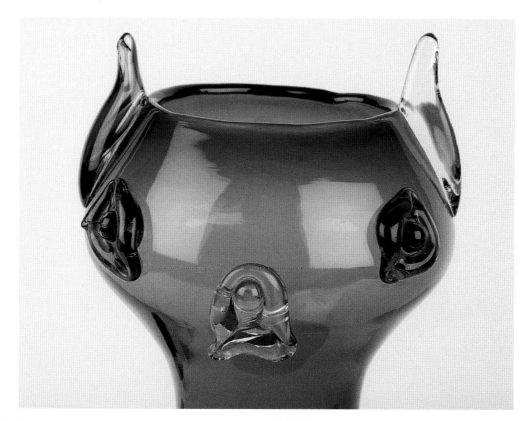

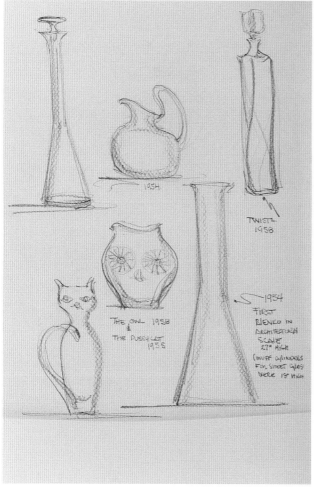

Top: Detail.

Bottom left: Husted's drawings with owl and pussycat.

Bottom right: Catalog drawing of Kitty decanters with head stopper. *Courtesy of Blenko.*

BLENKO 1970

Top left: #7050 with owl and lady stopper. *Courtesy of Blenko.* $150-200 each.

Top right: #7050 Blenko blue and Olive Green bulls. *Courtesy of Blenko.* $150-200 each.

Bottom left: #7050 Honey and Aqua owls. *Courtesy of Blenko.* $150-200 each.

Bottom right: #7050 with Olive Green and Honey pictorial discs. *Courtesy of Blenko.* $100-125 each.

**Opposite page:**

Top left: Cover of 1970 catalog with #7050 decanters.

Top right: #7050 animal decanters. Myers, design 50. Olive Green horse and Ruby bull stoppers in 8-1/2" crystal bottle. *Courtesy of Blenko.* $150-200 each.

Bottom left: Detail of bull.

Bottom right: Detail of horse.

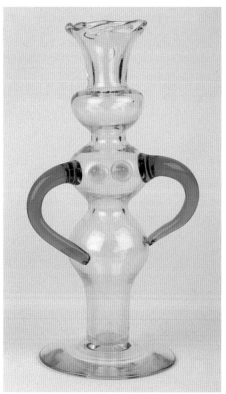

Top: Assortment of stoppers for #7050 decanter. *Courtesy of Blenko.*

Bottom left: #7047 nude. Myers 1970, design 47. Crystal with Sea Green trim vase/ewer in the form of a nude female with "Simpsons hairstyle" and hands on her hips. h. 11". *Courtesy of the Huntington.* $150-200.

Bottom center: #7047 nude in Crystal with Ruby. *Courtesy of Mitchell Attenson.* $150-200.

Bottom right: Detail.

Unidentified ladies, Crystal paperweights with Ruby facial features and hair styles. *Courtesy of Blenko.* $50-70 each.

Figural paperweights in Crystal with Ruby and Olive Green features. *Courtesy of Blenko.* $50-70 each.

Blenko blue goats. *Courtesy of Blenko.* $30-50 each.

Animal paperweights. *Courtesy of Blenko.*
$30-40 each.

Animal paperweights. *Courtesy of Blenko.*
$30-40 each.

Animal paperweights. *Courtesy of Blenko.*
$30-40 each.

Top left: Horse head on lid of canister. *Courtesy of Blenko.*

Top right: Photo of canister with horse head. *Courtesy of the Huntington.*

Bottom left: #7929 toad vase in Wheat, by Don Shepherd. h. 10-1/2". $50-75.

Bottom right: Back view.

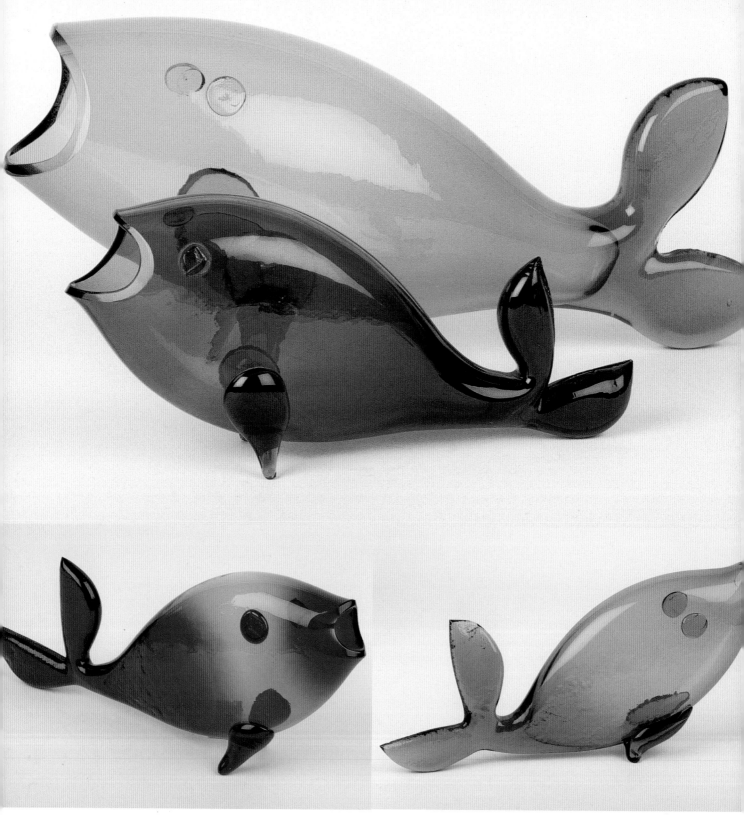

Top: #971-S fish vase in Amethyst with #971-M in Wheat, one of Anderson's best selling designs, c. 1950. l. 12-1/2" & 17". $50-60; $75-100.

Bottom left: Tangerine #971 fish vase. *Courtesy of Winslow Anderson*. $75-100.

Bottom right: Green #971 fish vase. *Courtesy of Winslow Anderson*. $75-100.

BLENKO HANDCRAFT

Piscatorial Pretties

These are the fish that *will* get away. Their colors, size range and decorative design for versatile use will *catch* the eye of many of your customers. They are Blenko handcrafted, available in six beautiful Blenko colors: Sea Green, Jonquil, Rosé, Crystal, Tangerine and Turquoise.

971-L 21" long

971-M 16" long

*Nationally Advertised*

971-S 12" long

5433 8" high

SALES OFFICES

RUBEL SALES COMPANY  JOHNSON SALES COMPANY  LEE HENNERY & ASSOCIATES
225 Fifth Avenue          1119 Trade Mart Building      Space 614-615
New York 10, N. Y.         Dallas, Texas                Atlanta Merchandise Mart
                                                        Atlanta 3, Georgia

RUBEL SALES COMPANY  DILLON-WELLS, INC.          FRANK K. SCHILLING
1554 Merchandise Mart   760 West Seventh Street      Box 416
Chicago, Illinois       Los Angeles 17, California    Butte, Montana

BLENKO GLASS COMPANY INCORPORATED
Milton, West Virginia

Top: #5433 fish vase. Husted 1954, design 33. Cobalt crackle fish, a variation of Anderson's earlier design. h. 10". $75-100.

Bottom left: Advertisement for fish vases. *Courtesy of Blenko.*

Bottom right: Advertisement with fish vases. *Courtesy of Blenko.*

189

Heavy molded decorative items in Tangerine and Honey. *Courtesy of Blenko.* $20-30 each.

Honey and green pears. *Courtesy of Winslow Anderson.* $25-35 each.

Crackle apple in Tangerine. $15-25.

Variety of blown fruit. *Courtesy of Blenko.* $25-35 each.

190

#9490 molded corn. l. 11". *Courtesy of Blenko.* $35-55.

#7020-M & #7020-L mushroom paperweights, similar to mushroom stoppers in decanters also designed by Myers in the 1970 line. h. 3" & 3-1/2". *Courtesy of Blenko.* $15-20; $20-25.

#7022-S mushroom decanter. Myers 1970, design 22. Mushroom paperweight stopper on small Tangerine decanter. h. 8-1/2". $60-80.

#7022-L large mushroom decanter, shown with small one to show relative size. h. 13-1/2". $100-125.

#8433 hats in Crystal, Olive Green, Turquoise, and Ruby. *Courtesy of Blenko.* $20-50 each.

Left: Small #930 Sky Blue hat and Crystal crackle with Sea Green raspberries. *Courtesy of the Huntington.* $20-25; $50-60.

Right: Crystal with deep green bell. h. 8". *Courtesy of Blenko.* $50-60.

#992 steer wall vase. Anderson c. 1951. Sea Green steer head wall pocket with long horns, recipient of the 1952 Good Design Award from the Museum of Modern Art. l. 21-1/2". *Courtesy of Blenko.* $175-225.

Top: #964-L horn vase. Anderson c. 1950. Tangerine long horn vase, a classic '50s Blenko form; with sandblast signature. l. 22". $150-175 (+signature).

Center left: Horn vases in Ruby and Chartreuse. l. 22". *Courtesy of Blenko.* $150-175 each.

Center right: #964-S short horn vases in Turquoise and Aqua, with large horn to show relative size. l. 18-1/2" & 22". *Courtesy of Blenko.* $75-125.

Bottom left: #964-S short horn vase in Charcoal and Crystal, but with curled tail variation; with green and Tangerine long horn vases. $75-125; $150-175 each.

Bottom right: Short horn vases in Jonquil, with long horn in blue gray. *Courtesy of Blenko.* $75-125 each; $150-175.

Left: Ruby cornucopia vase mounted on Crystal block base, not a production piece. *Courtesy of Blenko.*

Right: #5310 wall pockets. Anderson 1953, design 10. Freeform handkerchief vases in Crystal and Sea Green, no two made alike. *Courtesy of Winslow Anderson.* $75-100 each.

Left: "Holy Family" casting in Honey, on wood base. h. 12". *Courtesy of Attenson Antiques.* $100-125.

Right: #6318 Turquoise bookends in large teardrop shape. h. 6-1/4". *Courtesy of Blenko.* $100-150 pair.

Left: Turquoise head vase, by Don Shepherd in late 1970s. h. 12". *Courtesy of Blenko.* $75-100.

Right: #51 blown bubbles in 3", 4-1/2", and 6" sizes and various colors. $10-25 each.

# PART THREE —PAST, PRESENT, FUTURE

## Chapter 11
# Past: 1960 Catalog

The first full color catalog was produced in 1959 by Wayne Husted. Since the year 1960 falls in the middle of the two most collectible decades of Blenko glass, and since this catalog is one of only two years in color not already reproduced in a publication (the other is 1961), I have included it here to represent "the past." Unusual lines—Raindrops, Regal, and Rialto—were made, with few exceptions, exclusively in 1960. Because of their relative scarcity, even the Huntington and Blenko museums lacked examples in their collections to photograph for this volume. Therefore, these catalog pages can serve both as historical documents for researchers and identification tools for collectors.

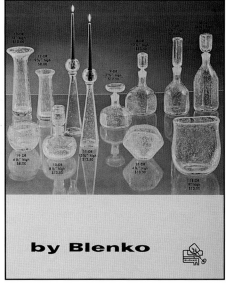

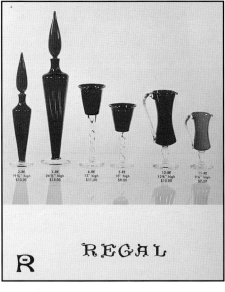

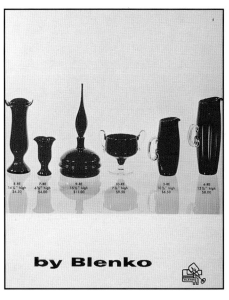

| 15-TO 9½" high $6.50 | 14-TO 8¾" high $5.50 | 2-TO 18½" high $10.00 | 5-TO 17" high $9.00 | 6-TO 14" high $7.50 | 7-TO 9½" high $6.00 | 1-TO 20¼" high $12.00 |
|---|---|---|---|---|---|---|

| 10-TO 11" wide $9.00 | 9-TO 7¼" wide $6.00 | 13-TO 13¼" high $6.00 | 12-TO 8½" high $5.50 | 4-TO 14" high $11.00 | 3-TO 6" high $9.00 | 16-TO 8½" high $6.00 | 8-TO $6.00 |
|---|---|---|---|---|---|---|---|

# R  RIALTO  by Blenko

8

| *5519-L 16" high $7.50 | 489 13" high $12.00 | 5611 9¾" high $5.00 | 5433 10" high $12.00 | 5825-L 23" high $12.50 | 555 5" high $4.00 | 5825-S 19½" high $10.00 | 5941 13" high $8.00 |
|---|---|---|---|---|---|---|---|

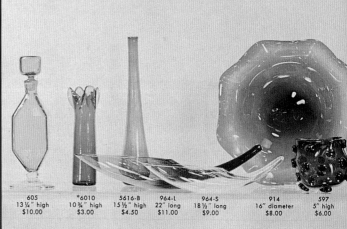

| 605 13¼" high $10.00 | *6010 10¾" high $3.00 | 5616-B 15½" high $4.50 | 964-L 22" long $11.00 | 964-S 18½" long $9.00 | 914 16" diameter $8.00 | 597 5" high $6.00 |
|---|---|---|---|---|---|---|

LILAC

| 5937 | 561 | 5616-C | 971-S | 971-L | 595 | *920-S | *920 | *920-L | 991 | 6026 | 596 | 601 | 602 |

**6034**
19" high
$9.00

**6031**
9" high
$4.50

**608**
8½" high
$3.50

**6039**
13½" high
$8.00

**6032**
10" high
$5.00

**6033**
4¾" high
$2.00

**538**
4" high
$4.00

**6016**
3" high
$4.00

**6017**
3" high
$3.50

**6035**
5" high
$4.00

***6030-S**
10½" high
$5.00

***6030-M**
13" high
$6.00

***6030-L**
18½" high
$7.50

**6039**
13½" high
$8.00

**606**
11½" high
$8.00

***6011**
4" high
$3.50

**6038**
13¾" high
$7.50

**6041**
10½" high
$5.00

**607**
10" high
$3.50

**5929-S**
22¼" high
$12.50

**5922-L**
19½" high
$10.00

**5922-S**
14¼" high
$7.00

***6014**
8" dia.
$3.50

**6046**
7½" high
$3.50

**609**
8¾" high
$3.50

**6018**
4" high
$5.00

***569**
13" high
$6.50

**603**
7" high
$4.00

***6025**
12" high
$3.00

***6024**
15¼" high
$4.00

**565**
10¾" high
$8.00

**413-L**
13" high
$9.00

***5519-M**
11¼" high
$6.00

**537**
10" length
$3.50

***388**
7½" high
$5.50

***390**
8" high
$4.50

***413-S**
8" high
$7.00

***366-M**
9½" high
$5.00

***366-S**
7" high
$4.00

***366-L**
12" high
$6.50

**384**
7½" high
$3.00

**976**
19½" high
$10.00

**5917 Bowl**
13" dia.
$5.00

**5919 Vase**
7¾" high
$5.00

**990-A**
½" dia.

***418-L**
6" high

***418-S**
4½" high

**5918 Bowl**
15¼" dia.

**59 Crystals**
$1.00 per box

**472 Nuggets**
$1.50 box

**434**
5½" high

***5318**
7½" high

**B-508**
6½" dia.

**452**
6½" dia.

**993**
7" dia.

**5920**
10" high

***546**
10¾" high

**5816-L**
15" high

**5816-S**
8" high

*366-LL
12" high
$7.50

*366-SL
7" high
$5.00

*366-ML
9½" high
$6.00

*37
13" high
$6.00

564
18¼" high
$8.00

604
15" high
$6.00

*3716
11" dia.
$4.50

*3744-X
7" dia.
$3.50

*5431
12¾" long
$5.00

5940
7" high
$7.00

*939-P
14¼" high
$7.00

*5913
14" high
$8.00

*49
10½" high
$6.00

*404-M
11½" high
$7.00
*404-L
(not shown)
15" high
$11.00

5926-L
12½" high
$10.00

5926-S
9" high
$6.00

5931
14" high
$7.00

593
8" dia.
$4.00

*361-P
7½" high
$5.50

*3750-L
5½" high
$4.50

955-L
17½" long
$7.50

51-L
6" dia.
$18.00 doz.

51
3" dia.
$9.00 doz.

*533
7" high
$3.00

*5429
11" long
$5.00

5932
15" high
$9.00

*543
7¼" high
$4.50

*948
13" high
$6.50

5933
16¼" high
$9.00

5815-S
17" high
$8.00

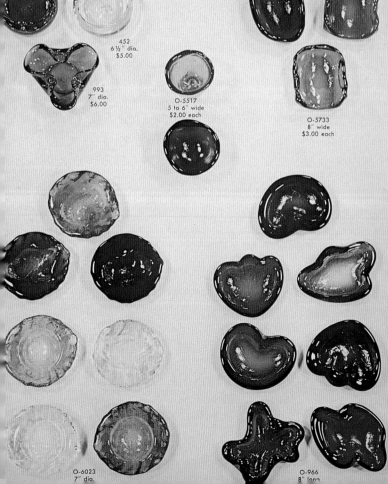

508
6½" dia.
$6.00

452
6½" dia.
$5.00

993
7" dia.
$6.00

O-5517
5 to 6" wide
$2.00 each

O-5733
8" wide
$3.00 each

O-6023
7" dia.

O-966
8" long

TANGERINE

JONQUIL

PERSIAN

SEA GREEN

TUR

5516
32" high
$22.50
with Stopper
$25.00

588
30" high
$17.50

587-L
37" high
$17.50

*6029
28" high
$12.50

5415
27" high
$20.00

5717
24" high
$12.00

# Chapter 12

# Present: Matt Carter

Blenko's first designer Winslow Anderson, with latest designer Matthew Carter, May 1998. *Photo Courtesy of Matt Carter.*

The glass objects made at Blenko are a combination of the designer's imagination and the skilled hands of the craftsman who transforms the molten liquid into a shimmering solid. The hand method of manufacture we use creates a completely different product from machine-made glass.

We do not use mechanized forming and finishing machines. Once the craftsman has initially shaped the glass object, it is then transferred to a pontil rod and finished entirely by hand. The pontil mark on the bottom of each piece of glass is one of the distinctive marks that reveals our handmade process.

Because our glass is made in small batches and our processes are all operated by hand, it is common to find bubbles, lines, and the individual marks of the craftsman in all our products. These are not flaws but rather the distinctive marks of a handmade object.

Automated machines turn out tremendous quantities of glass pieces daily which are exactly alike and without character. In a world of standardization, we recognize the repetition and dullness that threatens our own individuality. For this reason we all need, more than ever before, handmade objects that are unique and inspiring.

*—from the Blenko catalogs*

## Matthew Carter

Beginning in 1995 Matt Carter was the designer in charge of carrying out the Blenko philosophy and tradition. Also a skilled glassblower, Carter understands the material—its capabilities and its limits. Equally as important, he loves his work.

If you would have asked me when I was a kid what I would be doing, I wouldn't have thought of this. I remember going to visit glass studios with my grandparents in Rhode Island and thinking how fascinating it was, but never in my wildest dreams did I think I would be doing this for a living. I still catch myself watching the craftsmen at Blenko make one or several of my designs, and I mentally have to pinch myself. I am getting paid to do something that I love to do, and how many people get to say that every day?

*—Matt Carter*

*The following is excerpted (with minor editions) from typescripts by Carter.*

I was born in Manchester, Connecticut, in 1970. While studying to be a high school history teacher, I needed a three-credit-hour class to substitute for a history course that was not being offered. As I looked through the course offerings, I noticed a class in glassblowing. Needless to say, I fell in love with the material that first day, and I haven't looked back since.

In the summer of 1991 I worked as an assistant for glass artist John Fitzpatrick. As a studio technician/assistant from 1992-1994, I also had the opportunity to learn metal working with Anderson's artist-in-residence Ken Ryden. Also between 1992 and 1994, I worked as an assistant and glass designer for the Bayliss Design Group. In July of 1993, my internship was at Blenko Glass Co, where I worked under the direction of Hank Murta Adams. When I graduated from Anderson University in Anderson, Indiana, in May of 1994, I went to Stanwood, Washington, to study briefly at the famous Pilchuck Glass School.

Since working for Blenko, in addition to my responsibilities as Design Director, I have designed and produced sales catalogs, overseen production and quality control of the glass recipes and the seven blowing shops, and represented Blenko to sales agents and major clients. Being a glassblower myself, I find it difficult at times to watch my designs being executed, because I want to jump in and work the material myself. And sometimes I can do that, when we are working with new samples. But being able to step back and watch the piece being made also gives me a perspective that I don't get while sitting at the bench. By observing the process, I am able to take in the bigger picture and see things that I wouldn't be able to see if I was making the piece.

I am fortunate to be surrounded by skilled craftsmen who are able to transform this molten material into a beautiful piece of glass. When I come up with a new design, I know that it is in capable hands. This relationship between designer and craftsman (gaffer) is very important. The designer must be able to communicate through drawings and through the glass. And throughout the process, we are a team. I may be the choreographer, but the dance requires total teamwork, communication, and timing. Each "dancer" has a specific part at a specific time, and without this the piece is lost. Timing is everything with glass.

Each piece is a reflection of the people who made it possible—from designer, to gaffer/craftsmen, to the customer. It is a reflection of the care and love of the craft that keeps me going back for more. It is also the adventure of making a piece of glass, because I always try to leave some part of my design open—open to show me something that may be better than my original concept. Not only must I listen to the glass tell me what it wants to do, I must also listen to the people—craftsmen, sales reps, customers, and critics, especially Mom. And again, timing is important—to know when to listen and when to go with an idea because I like what is happening. Design is all about process. And glass design is also about fun. I have to enjoy what I am doing or it will show up in my work. Imagine that.

*The following studio work was designed and blown by Matt Carter. Photos by George Abaid are courtesy of Matt Carter.*

Matt Carter, William Blenko Jr., Wayne Husted, and Richard Blenko outside with the piles of cullet, summer 1999.

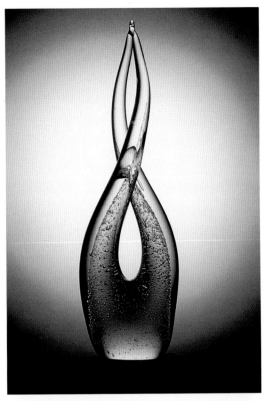

Top left: Matt Carter, "Twist," 1993; h. 24".
*Collection of Bill & Gloria Gaither.*

Center left: Cut and polished bowl, with paradise paints, 1994; h. 8".

Bottom left: Bowl on crystal and cobalt donut paperweight base, 1993; h. 8"; d. 17".

Top right: Crystal stemware, "Rockets," 1994.

Center right: Sandblasted glass sculpture, "Match Box," 1994.

Bottom right: Crystal stemware, "Bugles," 1994.

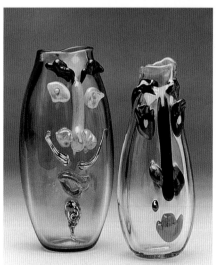  

Top: Decanter study made for Blenko, 1998.

Bottom left: Portrait vases, "King Leer & his Wife," 1994.

Bottom center: Portrait vases, "Salvador Dali" and "Tammy Faye," 1994.

Bottom right: Cut and polished crystal vase made for Blenko, 1998.

Top left: Cobalt blue collection, made for Blenko, 1996.

Top right: Violet fluted bowl with crystal trim, made for Blenko, 1997.

Bottom left: Cobalt and kiwi footed bowls, made for Blenko, 1998.

Bottom right: Cobalt bowl with crystal foot, made for Blenko, 1997.

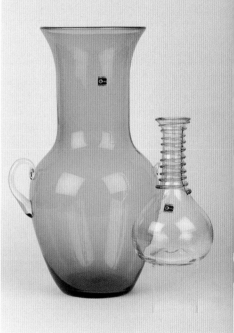

Top left: #9622 vase. Carter 1999, design 22. Cobalt vase with Crystal foot and handles. h. 14-1/2". *Courtesy of Blenko.*

Top center: Sample 1999 decanter in Azure Blue and Crystal, h. 18". *Courtesy of Blenko.*

Top right: "Designer's Studio Series" signature vase in Cobalt with Kiwi handles, designed by Carter in 1999 and signed by Richard Blenko. *Courtesy of Blenko.*

Center left: #9922-L vase. Carter 1999, design 22. Cobalt vase with ball stem and Crystal foot. h. 18".

Center: #9925 vase. Carter 1999, design 25. Cobalt globular vase with turned rim. h. 11-12". *Courtesy of Blenko.*

Center right: #9917 & #9432 vases. Carter 1999, design 17; Gibbons 1994, design 32. Large Kiwi vase with Crystal handles; Crystal crackle bottle/vase with applied Kiwi spiral.

Bottom: #9812 vases. Carter 1998, design 12. Kiwi crackle vases in mushroom form with extending rim. h. 8-1/4".

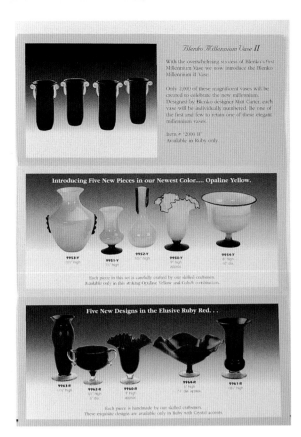

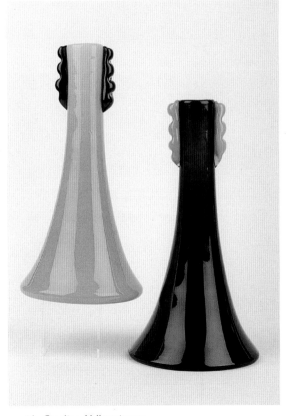

Top left: Page from Blenko 1999 brochure with Opaline Yellow items.

Top right: #9953-Y. Carter 1999, design 53. Opaline Yellow vase with applied Cobalt wings. h. 10-1/2".

Bottom left: Carter's Opaline Yellow vase with abstract Cobalt decoration.

Bottom right: Carter's Opaline Yellow and Cobalt candle holders.

# Chapter 13
# Future

As the white-haired wild-eyed scientist Dr. Emmett Brown (played by Christopher Lloyd) tells Marty (played by Michael J. Fox) in the film *Back to the Future II,* "...of course the page is blank—the future hasn't been written yet." And just as it was up to Marty to make his own destiny, it will be up to Blenko's leadership, designers, and craftsmen to determine theirs.

# Selected Bibliography

Alford, Judy. *Collecting Crackle Glass*. Atglen, Pennsylvania: Schiffer Publishing Ltd., 1995.

Anderson, Winslow. *Off-Hand Glass for Production. New American Glass: Focus West Virginia*. Huntington, West Virginia: Huntington Galleries, [1976].

———. handwritten biographical material. 1999.

Blenko Glass Company catalogs 1940s-1999.

———. archives, Milton, West Virginia.

Carter, Matt. Typescript of biographical material. 1999.

Corning Museum of Glass. *Glass 1959*. Corning, New York: Corning Museum, 1959.

"Crackle Glass Heating Up." *Antique Trader's Collector Magazine* (Sept 1996): 7.

Eige, Eason, & Rick Wilson. *Blenko Glass: 1930-1953*. Marietta, OH: Antique Publications, 1987.

Eige, Eason. *A Century of Glassmaking in West Virginia*. Huntington, West Virginia: Huntington Galleries, 1980.

Grayson, June. "Crackle Glass." *Glass Collector's Digest* (Oct/Nov 1989): 50-55.

Husted, Wayne. Typescripts and e-mail of biographical material, archival photographs, and drawings, 1999.

*Joel Philip Myers*. Exhibit catalog. Cleveland: Riley Hawk Galleries, 1992.

"Joel Philip Myers." Exhibit brochure of Retrospective Exhibition 1969 to 1999. New York: Barry Friedman, Ltd., 1999.

*Joel Philip Myers: Dialogues, Enticements and Color Studies*. Exhibit catalog. Chicago: Marx-Saunders Gallery, Ltd., 1999.

Lynggaard, Finn. *Joel Philip Myers*. Exhibit catalog. Ebeltoft, Denmark: Glasmuseum, 1993.

Metropolitan Museum of Art. *Twentieth Century Glass: American and European*. New York: Metropolitan Museum, 1950.

Myers, Joel Philip. Typescript of biographical material, 1999.

Piña, Leslie. *Popular '50s & '60s Glass: Color Along the River*. 2nd Edition. Atglen, Pennsylvania: Schiffer Publishing Ltd., 2005.

———, *Crackle Glass Too*, Atglen, Pennsylvania: Schiffer Publishing Ltd., 2002.

———, *Crackle Glass in Color*, Atglen, Pennsylvania: Schiffer Publishing Ltd., 2000.

———. *Blenko Glass 1962-1971 Catalogs*. Atglen, Pennsylvania: Schiffer Publishing Ltd., 2000.

———. *circa Fifties Glass from Europe & America*. Atglen, Pennsylvania: Schiffer Publishing Ltd., 1997.

Szymanski, Sylvia D. "Williamsburg Reproductions." *Glass Collector's Digest* 5 (Ap/May 1992): 50-54.

Wilson, Rick. "We're In For It: Early Days at Blenko Glass." *Goldenseal: West Virginia Traditional Life* 13 (Fall 1987): 43-49.

———. "Blenko Glass: An Inside Story." *Glass Collector's Digest* 1 (Oct/Nov 1987): 73-82.

———. "Winslow Anderson." *Glass Collector's Digest* 2 (June/July 1988): 26-33.

Witek, John & Deborah Novak. *Hearts of Glass: The Story of Blenko Handcraft*. Video. Witek & Novak, Inc. for West Virginia Public Television, 1998.

Yood, James. "Joel Philip Myers." *American Craft* (Aug/Sept 1999): 40-43.

## Personal interviews

Winslow Anderson, June 1999.

Richard Blenko, June 1999.

William Blenko Jr., June 1999.

Matthew Carter, June 1999.

Wayne Husted, June 1999 & 2001.

Joel Myers (telephone interview), November 1999.

# Designer Index

Adams, Hank, 19, 20, 24, 25

Anderson, Winslow, 26-32, 52, 78, 81, 88, 89, 92, 96, 105-110, 112-115, 118, 123-127, 130-133, 139-144, 151, 156-161, 163-167, 169-171, 173, 175-179, 188, 192-194

Carter, Matt, 20, 21, 25, 199-205

Husted, Wayne, 21, 33-40, 48, 51-68, 73-77, 81, 84-87, 91, 93, 98, 99, 101-103, 119, 121, 123, 124, 127, 129, 130, 134, 135, 138, 160, 163, 166-169, 171, 180, 181, 189, 195-198

Myers, Joel, 41-47, 49-51, 53, 54, 58, 59 63-65, 68-70, 77-83, 83, 88-91, 98, 99, 110-112, 115, 122, 130, 136, 137, 139, 160-162, 174, 182-184, 191

Nickerson, John, 71, 72, 82, 85, 167, 169

Shepherd, Don, 16-18, 22, 23, 92, 161, 187, 194